NEW DIRECTIONS FOR EVALUATION
A PUBLICATION OF THE AMERICAN EVALUATION ASSOCIATION

Gary T. Henry, *Georgia State University*
COEDITOR-IN-CHIEF

Jennifer C. Greene, *University of Illinois*
COEDITOR-IN-CHIEF

The Art, Craft, and Science of Evaluation Capacity Building

Donald W. Compton
American Cancer Society

Michael Baizerman
University of Minnesota

Stacey Hueftle Stockdill
EnSearch, Inc.

EDITORS

Number 93, Spring 2002

JOSSEY-BASS
San Francisco

THE ART, CRAFT, AND SCIENCE OF EVALUATION CAPACITY BUILDING
Donald W. Compton, Michael Baizerman, Stacey Hueftle Stockdill (eds.)
New Directions for Evaluation, no. 93
Jennifer C. Greene, Gary T. Henry, Coeditors-in-Chief
Copyright ©2002 Wiley Periodicals, Inc., A Wiley company

Microfilm copies of issues and articles are available in 16mm and 35mm, as well as microfiche in 105mm, through University Microfilms Inc., 300 North Zeeb Road, Ann Arbor, Michigan 48106-1346.

New Directions for Evaluation is indexed in Contents Pages in Education, Higher Education Abstracts, and Sociological Abstracts.

Print ISSN: 1097-6736; Online ISSN: 1534-875X ISBN: 0-7879-6299-6

NEW DIRECTIONS FOR EVALUATION is part of The Jossey-Bass Education Series and is published quarterly by Wiley Subscription Services, Inc., a Wiley company, at Jossey-Bass, 989 Market Street, San Francisco, California 94103-1741.

SUBSCRIPTIONS cost $69.00 for U.S./Canada/Mexico; $93 international. For institutions, agencies, and libraries, $145 U.S.; $185 Canada; $219 international. Prices subject to change.

EDITORIAL CORRESPONDENCE should be addressed to the Editors-in-Chief, Jennifer C. Greene, Department of Educational Psychology, University of Illinois, 260E Education Building, 1310 South Sixth Street, Champaign, IL 61820, or Gary T. Henry, School of Policy Studies, Georgia State University, P.O. Box 4039, Atlanta, GA 30302-4039.

www.josseybass.com

Editorial Policy and Procedures

New Directions for Evaluation, a quarterly sourcebook, is an official publication of the American Evaluation Association. The journal publishes empirical, methodological, and theoretical works on all aspects of evaluation. A reflective approach to evaluation is an essential strand to be woven through every volume. The editors encourage volumes that have one of three foci: (1) craft volumes that present approaches, methods, or techniques that can be applied in evaluation practice, such as the use of templates, case studies, or survey research; (2) professional issue volumes that present issues of import for the field of evaluation, such as utilization of evaluation or locus of evaluation capacity; (3) societal issue volumes that draw out the implications of intellectual, social, or cultural developments for the field of evaluation, such as the women's movement, communitarianism, or multiculturalism. A wide range of substantive domains is appropriate for *New Directions for Evaluation;* however, the domains must be of interest to a large audience within the field of evaluation. We encourage a diversity of perspectives and experiences within each volume, as well as creative bridges between evaluation and other sectors of our collective lives.

The editors do not consider or publish unsolicited single manuscripts. Each issue of the journal is devoted to a single topic, with contributions solicited, organized, reviewed, and edited by a guest editor. Issues may take any of several forms, such as a series of related chapters, a debate, or a long article followed by brief critical commentaries. In all cases, the proposals must follow a specific format, which can be obtained from the editor-in-chief. These proposals are sent to members of the editorial board and to relevant substantive experts for peer review. The process may result in acceptance, a recommendation to revise and resubmit, or rejection. However, the editors are committed to working constructively with potential guest editors to help them develop acceptable proposals.

Jennifer C. Greene, Coeditor-in-Chief
Department of Educational Psychology
University of Illinois
260E Education Building
1310 South Sixth Street
Champaign, IL 61820
e-mail:jcgreene@uiuc.edu

Gary T. Henry, Coeditor-in-Chief
School of Policy Studies
Georgia State University
P.O. Box 4039
Atlanta, GA 30302-4039
e-mail: gthenry@gsu.edu

CONTENTS

Editors' Notes

This volume represents a first mapping of evaluation capacity building (ECB) as a process, an occupational orientation, and a practice—part art, part craft, and part science. In ten years, perhaps Stufflebeam will prepare a volume on ECB as he did when he compared models (Stufflebeam, 2001). By then, if we are successful, more ECB will have been published and practiced. Although ECB is being carried out now, it is often taken for granted and hence is invisible, not noticed, not named as distinct, intentional work.

In this volume, we make an important conceptual distinction: ECB processes and practices are different from yet show a resemblance to program evaluation processes and practices. This point cannot be overemphasized. We want this distinction to be clear and open to analysis and discussion, with the possibility that ECB can be seen and accepted as a legitimate focus within the evaluation community. This distinction has real, immediate, and practical consequences for whether and how organizations, programs, governments, and communities take on and sustain evaluation and its uses as ordinary, everyday practices. These distinctions are seen in our working definition of ECB: *ECB is the intentional work to continuously create and sustain overall organizational processes that make quality evaluation and its uses routine.*

This does *not* mean that we expect all program evaluators to take on ECB practices as such, only that we want ECB to be viewed as a legitimate professional role with explicit responsibilities, tasks, skills, and behaviors.

We offer three examples to help clarify the distinctions we are making between the program evaluation practitioner and the ECB practitioner. In the first example, we start with the most common and straightforward way of understanding ECB.

> A former University of Minnesota student asked coeditor Stockdill, a private evaluation practitioner, if evaluation skills could be taught to middle managers at The Mayo Foundation sites in Rochester, Minnesota, and Scottsdale, Arizona. The purpose was to help these middle managers learn basic evaluation skills such as identifying evaluation projects, stakeholders, and questions;

We would like to acknowledge colleagues who helped us construct this volume. Gary Henry, coeditor-in-chief, accepted our idea and encouraged its development. Patricia Rieker, Simmons College and Harvard Medical School, showed a special acuity in reading draft text and was always helpful and supportive. Marlene Stoehr was a skilled editor who helped make our work clearer and more robust. Ross VeLure Roholt provided considerable and greatly appreciated technical support and assistance.

To the authors of the case studies, we owe heartfelt thanks for their trust in our conception and for their skillful and timely work.

determining the most appropriate methods for answering the evaluation questions; developing the data-collection tools; collecting the information; analyzing the information; and using the information to make decisions. During the training, managers identified and developed evaluation plans for a number of projects. One was to evaluate an educational training program on managing diabetes for newly diagnosed diabetics; another was to evaluate an innovative technology designed to enhance the communication between the supply room and surgical unit. The focus of the training was to teach the skills of evaluation—to add evaluation skills to the toolkit of middle managers at these Mayo sites.

This example illustrates the typical way that ECB is viewed. In this example, the evaluation practitioner is the middle manager. From our perspective, this is *not* an ECB example because no one had primary responsibility for ensuring that evaluation work would be sustained and become a regular, ongoing practice of the organization.

In the next example, we see an external evaluator taking on an evaluation practitioner role and an ECB practitioner role.

The client, Lifetrack Resources, wanted a formative and summative evaluation of a program designed to help individuals make a transition from welfare to work. Stockdill worked from the evaluation practitioner's perspective to identify other stakeholders, identify the formative and summative evaluation questions, identify the methods that would best answer those questions, and develop an evaluation plan for this two-year project. She worked with staff to collect qualitative and quantitative data and provided ongoing feedback so that program strengths could be built upon and weaknesses addressed.

The focus for the ECB practitioner is on an intentional action system of guided processes and practices for bringing about and sustaining a state of affairs in which quality evaluation and its appropriate uses are ordinary and ongoing practices within and/or between one or more organizations/programs/sites. ECB, rather than program evaluation, became the work at Lifetrack Resources when Stockdill was asked to give advice on how to integrate various evaluation initiatives. The Lifetrack Resources board of directors had a continuous quality improvement committee, a customer focus committee, and a strategic planning committee. The program staff, because of United Way funding, had identified program outcomes and provided this funder with outcome data, as well as information regarding what was learned and how these learnings had been used to improve practice. The administrative team wanted to know how to learn from the practices used to complete the formative and summative evaluations; the outcome evaluation; and the board-initiated continuous quality improvement effort, customer focus, and strategic planning efforts and how to integrate these efforts so that, instead of carrying out disparate and unrelated activities, the agency could become a learning organization. In this work, Stockdill became a resource on ECB practice for the agency's administrative team, who became ECB practitioners.

The third example shows the distinction we make between the program evaluation practitioner and the ECB practitioner from an organizational perspective. The distinction is made clearer in Chapter Four, where the authors describe ECB practice at the American Cancer Society (ACS).

> From the program evaluation practitioner's perspective, developing and sustaining an evaluation unit within an organization focuses primarily on the finite task at hand. Typically, this means responding to the next request to conduct a study, standardizing data-collection instruments for use by multiple clients, and ensuring their use of the evaluation findings. In this way, developing and sustaining the unit is seen as responding to the demand for evaluation in the moment. Less attention is given to the larger goal of systematically creating ways for evaluation and its uses to be seen as regular practices throughout the organization.
>
> For the ECB practitioner, however, the focus is on responding to requests for evaluation services while being mindful of how today's work will contribute to the sustentation of the unit in the longer term. This dual role might be thought of as "wearing bifocals" that allow a given situation to be assessed differently by the program evaluation practitioner and the ECB practitioner. Put differently, in interactions with a client the evaluation practitioner asks the question, "How will this contribute to making this a better study and make use more likely and make possible another quality study?" The ECB practitioner asks, "How will this moment in this particular evaluation contribute to the organization's learning and development such that the next study will be asked for and used?" In this way, the ECB practitioner considers how each study is connected to the development of the organization and to meeting the organization's goals and mission.

These three examples are intended to locate your own practice. Which best characterizes your everyday work? In this volume, ECB is presented primarily from the perspective of internal evaluators working to build and sustain ongoing evaluation and its uses—the third example.

This is a volume for evaluation practitioners and for donors (foundation, government, United Way) and recipients (social agencies, not-for-profit organizations and other human services programs, schools) who want to know how to engage in effective ECB. This volume excludes certain material the reader might expect to find. There is no in-depth discussion of program evaluation and its practice, except to distinguish it from ECB. Any explicit assessment of particular ECB processes or practices are excluded, and there is no assessment of the case studies. No preference is stated regarding the best, correct, or most effective ECB efforts. Ours is the earlier task of locating and making ECB work explicit. The editors offer no privileged definition of evaluation, and each author states her or his own definition, as it was used in the case study.

No mainstream program evaluation literature is reviewed here, although some is cited. Relatively little is published that uses an ECB vocabulary and that focuses primarily on ECB as distinct from and in contrast to program evaluation practice. But there is a richly suggestive body of literature for ECB work in the international arena. We decided to bring this to the professional mainstream while asking readers to set aside the international aspect of the examples and to focus instead on structural and process similarities to their own sites, settings, and organizations.

The attentive reader of the whole volume will be able to

- Distinguish ECB practice from evaluation practice
- Understand what ECB looks like in practice and how it is carried out in four different organizational settings
- Begin acquiring an ECB vocabulary and a conceptual model of the ECB, and will be introduced to ECB indicators

We must be explicit regarding why we chose the case studies. We asked ourselves how to best find, invite, structure, and present case studies. All abstracts submitted to the ECB presidential strand of the 2000 American Evaluation Association (AEA) Annual Meeting were reviewed. From those, a list of authors and reported examples were chosen. The case studies are all "insider" narratives, written by professionals who were intentionally engaged in both evaluation and ECB. These particular studies represent a cross-section of public agencies and NGOs (nongovernmental organizations); local, national, and world-level organizations; education, health, and social development arenas; small, low-budget, and large-scale operations; a nonprofit, a governmental agency, a school district, and an international organization; and organizations with one staff person and others with several professionals.

In other words, we present a range of cases showing ECB similarities and differences:

- *ECB at the American Cancer Society.* This case was chosen because it represents a nonprofit, nationwide, federated organization and because the lead author, Don Compton, received the 2000 AEA Alva and Gunner Myrdal Award, in part for his ECB work.

- *ECB at the Centers for Disease Control and Prevention.* This case was chosen because it is a national, governmental organization doing its own ECB work and sharing it with state and local public health organizations. The lead author, Bobby Milstein, was the organizer of the 2000 AEA ECB presidential strand (Milstein and Cotton, 2000).

- *ECB at Anoka-Hennepin Independent School District 11.* This case was chosen because many AEA papers come from and much ECB practice is conducted at educational sites. The author, Jean King, directs a doctoral program in program evaluation at the University of Minnesota, College of Education and Human Development. The work reported was done during a university leave of absence.

• *ECB at the World Bank.* This case was chosen because the World Bank, an international organization, has a long history of ECB practice and has theorized and written about its work. This field of ECB practice may be unfamiliar to many readers, but the ECB work will likely resonate with their own, however large the scale of the World Bank in comparison. This case study provides the perspective of ECB at the World Bank, its ECB outreach to developing nations, and how ECB works at those sites.

Some additional points to keep in mind when reading this volume are as follows:

• ECB is not in the everyday work world of most internal and external evaluators who do not have responsibility for facilitating ECB processes.
• Most ECB processes are a part of international social and economic development activities and in formal organizations, including governmental agencies. Many readers who are evaluation practitioners may understand the day-to-day operations of these sites but may not have an organizational conceptual framework within which they can easily place ECB.
• The case studies are insider narratives. The goal was to conceptualize and link them to theoretical issues about organizational learning and organizational development.
• The overarching belief of the editors is that ECB is easily demystified in its process, practices, occupational orientation, and practitioner roles. Evaluators and ECB practitioners both should find the material accessible, interesting, informative, and inviting.

It is our hope that ECB will be enhanced by this volume and that a more mature conceptualization and quality of ECB work will come from thoughtful and explicit practice, assessment, and evaluation of this practice and from the ongoing discussion.

Michael Baizerman
Donald W. Compton
Stacey Hueftle Stockdill
Editors

References

Milstein, B., and Cotton, D. "Defining Concepts for the Presidential Strand on Building Evaluation Capacity." [On-line at eval.org/eval2000/presstrand.htm.]
Stufflebeam, D. L. *Evaluation Models.* New Directions for Evaluation, no. 89. San Francisco: Jossey-Bass, 2001.

MICHAEL BAIZERMAN is a professor in the School of Social Work and adjunct professor in the College of Education and Human Development and in the School of Public Health at the University of Minnesota, St. Paul.

DONALD W. COMPTON is director of the Division of Evaluation Services, American Cancer Society, National Home Office, Atlanta.

STACEY HUEFTLE STOCKDILL is founder and CEO of EnSearch, Inc., a specialized evaluation firm in St. Paul, Minnesota.

1

The authors use the literature to develop conceptual and working definitions of ECB and use them to present a frame for reading the four case studies.

Toward a Definition of the ECB Process: A Conversation with the ECB Literature

Stacey Hueftle Stockdill, Michael Baizerman, Donald W. Compton

In this chapter, we present a beginning ECB vocabulary and a review of the relatively small ECB literature and what it teaches us for everyday practice. Next, in Chapters Two, Three, Four, and Five, we illustrate ECB practice through four case studies. In Chapters Six and Seven, we bring the volume together by explicating and integrating the theory, literature, and case study themes; we propose a beginning ECB framework and indicators.

ECB Defined

We intentionally place a *conceptual* definition of ECB at the beginning of the volume to provide a frame through which to engage the subject, the distinctions we make, and the case studies. We do this because the two major confusions in grasping and understanding ECB are (1) what it is and (2) the ways it is like and unlike program evaluation practice. We do this also for the following five reasons. We want to

- Make our understanding of ECB explicit
- Make the distinction between ECB and evaluation clear
- Encourage reflections by practitioners about how ECB relates to and informs their work and how it does not

- Stimulate discussions about differences between ECB and mainstreaming
- Stimulate thinking about relevant theoretical literature from other disciplines

We first present our conceptual definition of ECB and then contrast it to quality evaluation practice. Once the conceptual basis of ECB is presented, we provide a practical, *working* definition for the volume.

Toward a Conceptual Definition of ECB. ECB is *a context-dependent, intentional action system of guided processes and practices for bringing about and sustaining a state of affairs in which quality program evaluation and its appropriate uses are ordinary and ongoing practices within and/or between one or more organizations/programs/sites.*

By *context-dependent* we mean that whether and how ECB is carried out depends on the realities of each particular organizational site.

By an *intentional action system* we mean that ECB is done in an organization, program, or site by joining with others in ongoing collaboration and other forms of alliances and political relationships that, over time, show regularities that can be presented as purposive systems.

Guided refers to facilitating the creation and sustentation of the ECB action system; however, ECB practitioners rarely fully control the ECB process; they must continuously co-create opportunities for ECB.

The term *process* refers to the overall intentional effort to create and sustain an ECB action system. For example, each of the case studies shows an overall ECB process. In the American Cancer Society (ACS) case, the ECB process focused around crafting an evaluation framework for the national organization that included utilization-focused evaluation (UFE), the Joint Committee's standards (Joint Committee on Standards for Education Evaluation, 1994; hereafter "Joint Committee's standards"), a model of intra- and interorganizational collaboration, and a conception of organizational learning and development. Foci included developing and sustaining an evaluation unit, creating capacity to do evaluations, and developing the use of evaluation throughout the organization.

By *practices* we mean everyday ways of carrying out ECB. In the Centers for Disease Control and Prevention (CDC) case study, examples are given of meetings held, position papers written, and trainings provided. Their story tells how and why they worked as they did, "in the moment," intentionally and reflectively.

By *bringing about* we mean creating and sustaining the state of affairs in which evaluations are used now and will be used in the future. Sustaining ECB is a project never completed. There can always be a demand for another evaluation to be done and used; sustentation of ECB is never guaranteed. The evaluation unit can be closed and the ECB practitioners terminated.

By *state of affairs* we mean all that is seemingly necessary in a particular organization for evaluation work to be done and used. This includes organizational or program infrastructures, social norms, and practices;

cultural meanings and discourses; appropriately knowledgeable and skilled practitioners; and the other resources, structures, policies, rules, processes, and practices of quality evaluation.

Within and/or between one or more organizations/programs/sites refers to intra- and interorganizational contexts and programs, as well as sites such as a communities, collaborative partners, or other collectivities or social formations.

In the case studies, examples are given of both pure and mixed sites. For example, the national home office (NHO) of the ACS, as well as its regional offices and community-level units, are all ECB sites, with different ECB processes being undertaken by many practitioners. Pure and mixed sites are also seen in the CDC case study, in the school case study, and especially in the World Bank example.

Quality program evaluation means the expert and professional practice of evaluation carried out following the Joint Committee's standards and other relevant and appropriate guides, where *program evaluation* means accepted models and practices such as those reported by Stufflebeam (2001).

By *appropriate uses* we mean the multiple ways any evaluation can be used over time by stakeholders and others, including conceptual, process, and instrumental uses. For example, the same study can be used in many ways over time for different purposes.

Ordinary practices mean that the ECB process attempts to bring about "regular" and more or less accepted ways that evaluation work is done. These processes can become mundane and taken for granted—even invisible, unnoticed, and unreflected upon. Once institutionalized as an ordinary "way we do things around here," we can say that evaluation and its uses have been mainstreamed.

To better understand our conceptual definition, we ask that you consider the following examples:

• When a particular evaluation study is completed and used, what is left? What remains might be a new perspective on a service program, a new way of involving field staff, or a new logic model for the organization.

• Four expert evaluators come to an organization and, under contract, complete four evaluations of programs and processes and work with the stakeholders to use the evaluation and its findings to think about their work, to examine organization and program policy, to change how a program is organized or targeted, and the like. Their work having been done and the terms of their contract met, they leave.

• The four expert evaluators all work on salary for the same organization and take on four program evaluations, which they develop and carry out with stakeholders in ways that meet the Joint Committee's standards and organizational guidelines, by using two different models of evaluation, both of which are acceptable to noted theorists such as Stufflebeam (2001). When their data come in, they analyze and reflect on it along with the stakeholders and, with them, continue working at using the evaluations. When all of this is over, these four internal evaluators go on and do other evaluations within the organization.

• The expert evaluator comes to work at her employing organization and starts her day by looking to see whether the HR office has begun to implement changes in what professional employees are assessed on, including now the quality of their participation in agency efforts to use the findings of evaluation studies in their everyday work. Later, she checks with the communications department on whether subscriptions to an evaluation newsletter for eight agency field employees have been sent. She takes a phone call from an evaluator in a state-level office and responds to seventy-five e-mails from program staff, collaborators, and other departments.

The first two examples are about evaluation work by evaluation practitioners; the last example is ECB.

ECB is constituted of three structural elements: the overall process, actual practices, and the occupational orientation and practitioner role. Each of these elements is used in this and the last chapters to organize ECB by level, activity, and actor so as to present a conceptual framework for theory and research, a practitioner's framework for understanding direct practice, a reader's frame for the case studies, and a framework for contrasting ECB to program evaluation. The diagram in Figure 1.1 treats ECB as a triangle, with each side necessary and all three sides interactive.

What are the major differences between the perspectives of program evaluation and ECB regarding the three structural elements of overall process, the actual practices, and the occupational orientation and practitioner role? Program evaluation and ECB are complementary and different ways of understanding and working in an organization. They are two ways of carrying out evaluation work on behalf of an organization.

At this point, we present only a few differences between ECB and evaluation practice (see Table 1.1); a more detailed contrast is given in the final chapter.

Clearly there are differences here. Are these differences real, and do they appear in practice, that is, in actual practitioner roles and tasks? Yes,

Figure 1.1. Overview of ECB

Table 1.1. Comparisons of Perspectives on Program Evaluation and ECB

	Program Evaluation Perspective	ECB Practitioner Perspective
Overall Process	Program evaluation is a process of systematically using a recognized model in accordance with at least the Joint Committee's standards to complete an agreed-upon program evaluation study.	ECB is a context-dependent, intentional action system of guided processes and practices for bringing about and sustaining a state of affairs in which quality program evaluation and its appropriate uses are ordinary and ongoing practices within and/or between one or more organizations/programs/sites.
Actual Practices	Doing quality program evaluations using acceptable models (for example, Stufflebeam, 2001).	Ongoing guided processes and practices for bringing about and sustaining a state of affairs in which quality program evaluation and its appropriate uses are ordinary and ongoing practices within and/or between one or more organizations/ programs/sites.
Occupational Orientation and Practitioner Role	Occupational orientation to carrying out a study and enhancing its likely uses according to the norm of the discipline/profession/field.	Occupational orientation to try to keep evaluation as a necessary everyday administrative part of an organization's structure, culture, and work practice internally and in relation to other entities in its environment.

these are substantive differences of great consequence for the evaluation field, for organizations, and for practitioners of program evaluation and ECB. Surely expert evaluators can take on ECB, but when they do their orientation must be to ECB *even when* they are *also* doing program evaluation studies. They must use dual vision and work on both levels. In this instance, the program evaluation practitioner who is taking on the role of ECB practitioner must practice within *both* orientations—to the specific evaluation and to how this specific program evaluation contributes to the ECB process within the larger organization and its policies, programs, and practices. Each orientation to the evaluation work and to the ECB work has different time, space, and activity horizons; each is a different order of political work and policies. Each uses the social, behavioral, and human sciences differently to inform the two roles, and each orients differently to the organization and its development.

ECB evaluators see their roles and work differently compared to evaluators with no involvement (for example, "I am just here to do the study") or with high involvement (for example, "I want them to use the information for organizational change"). ECB is intentional work on the organization as a system and on its structure, culture, and everyday practices, with the intent to create and sustain a home for professional expert program evaluation and its uses. One's frame can also be "organizational development," as practiced in particular fields such as organizational development itself, business, public health, or the social services. These distinctions in role orientation are seen in Table 1.2.

ECB is clearly oriented to *intraorganizational* structures, cultures, and everyday practices. These could include a youth-serving organization, a hospital, a small community-based organization, and a very large corporation. ECB also (as the case studies will show) can be *inter*organizational and *inter*program. For example, an agent of one organization can work with a nation (World Bank case); a public health expert can do ECB with a state health department (CDC case); and a school system can do ECB with its schools (Anoka-Hennepin Independent School District 11 case).

Table 1.2. Comparisons of the Program Evaluation Practitioner Role and the ECB Practitioner Role

Program Evaluation Practitioner	ECB Practitioner
• Has program knowledge and skills	• Imagines, conceptualizes, envisions, co-creates, and co-sustains a state of affairs in which evaluation and its use is ongoing
• Designs and carries out a program evaluation in a professional and expert manner adhering at a minimum to the Joint Committee's standards	
• Manages evaluations	• Holds a perspective on how every evaluation may contribute to sustaining the necessary state of affairs and works strategically to those ends
• Knows how to carry out an evaluation within an organization and its structure, culture, and politics as an internal or external evaluator	
• Facilitates learning among those participating in the evaluation	• Co-designs and makes ordinary the everyday practices necessary to sustain the state of affairs and to support each, every, and all discrete evaluation studies and their uses
• Facilitates the use of the evaluation	
• Works primarily within an organizational or program context	• Uses a long-term, open-ended process for making the organization or program a place in which program evaluation as such and each program evaluation study can be used to enhance organizational effectiveness
• Belongs to a community of expert evaluators	
• Orients toward doing a quality evaluation that is used	
• Orients to a politics of discrete studies, client needs, professional reputation, and so forth	• May belong to multiple occupational communities, including evaluators, managers, and executives
	• Orients outward toward co-creating and co-sustaining the necessary state of affairs for program studies and their uses
	• Orients to a politics of guiding and sustaining organizational change, learning, and development

Table 1.3. ECB Reflections

Questions	ECB Answers
How many evaluations of what type, done how, would have to be done to bring about ECB in and between organizations?	The answer is none because isolated, episodic, individual evaluations do not produce the ongoing state of affairs for continuing evaluation and its uses.
How can and does actual program evaluation practice in an organization hinder, deflect, or otherwise make effective ECB practice *less likely* in that organization?	The answer is that ongoing, unused, routinized evaluation such as Title 1 of the Education Act serves to preclude viable, practical, useful studies from the points of view of the local site.
What are the ECB occupational orientation skill sets (for example, cognitive-analytic, interpersonal, and political)? Can these skills be acquired by training, and what training pedagogy is most effective?	The answer is unclear. A useful next step would be to conduct research about what these skill sets are, using experience and drawing on other disciplines and professions.

To close this section, consider the questions in Table 1.3 by way of stimulating and focusing your reflections on ECB.

For us, there is not a single ECB process or practice; rather, we see families of processes and practices. We also put great emphasis on the ongoing, open-ended, and emergent nature of ECB work—sustaining evaluation and its uses.

Sustentation. ECB work is about the continuous sustentation of supportive organizational structures, cultures, and everyday practices. We use the term *sustentation* (sustain, sustainability, sustainment) to get at the ongoing intentional work necessary to ensure that evaluation studies and their uses continue to be asked for and carried out. This word emphasizes ECB as an actual process, whereas the word *sustain* invokes the passive. To us, ECB is the larger process that includes both the "building in" aspect of the *institutionalization* and the centering aspect of the *mainstreaming* process. ECB, unlike most evaluation practice, is neither linear nor sequential, with a single end product. Rather, it is never ending—like the circus performer who constantly spins the many plates on top of the pole she holds. ECB is far more jazzlike and improvisational than it is like classical ballet. Sustaining ECB requires doing the many tasks, phases, and stages of work out of order, as in an "infinite game" (Carse, 1986) of ever-emergent rules and players. Sustentation is a space where art, science, and craft meet in the intentional effort to carry on and use quality evaluation for organizational goal achievement and development.

Uses. ECB encompasses the many ways program evaluations can be used by stakeholders and others over time. These practices have been conceptualized by Patton (1997) and others. The major point is that use of an evaluation need not be a one-time activity but can become an ongoing process of several participants, in the present and into the future.

Working Definition. Taken together, the early presentation of the conceptual definition, the contrast in perspective and role between evaluation and ECB, and the summative questions and answers about ECB bring us to a practical, usable, and flexible *working definition:*

ECB is the intentional work to continuously create and sustain overall organizational processes that make quality evaluation and its uses routine.

Now that you have been introduced to the topic of ECB, we invite you to use this understanding to engage the ECB literature.

Evaluation Capacity Building: A Conversation with the Literature

There is an ECB literature, and to review it is to learn the biography of this practice and the several ways it is conceptualized and carried out, as well as the contexts of this work. Here we present a highly selective review of the limited ECB literature. ECB in international evaluation has a history based in evaluation capacity development (ECD). For all practical purposes, ECB and ECD are used interchangeably (Schaumburg-Müller, 1996). However, it should be noted that the ECD literature is an important contribution to understanding the overall ECB process, its everyday practices, and its major concepts.

ECB as Defined in the Literature. Bamberger (2000) provides background for understanding evaluation and its contrast to ECD in the field of international development:

> For the purposes of this discussion, development programs are defined as all social and economic programs in developing countries funded by multilateral and bilateral development agencies or by international nongovernment organizations (NGOs). These funding agencies normally require that their programs be evaluated. The evaluations may be conducted by the funding agency, the national agency administering the program being evaluated, or international or national consultants. The evaluation activities may be limited to specific projects or programs, or they may seek to develop national evaluation capacity to replicate the methods. [p. 96]

He goes on to describe how the terms *evaluation* and *monitoring* are used in this context:

> The term *evaluation* is used differently by different agencies and authors. Some distinguish between *monitoring* activities, which are conducted during project or program implementation to assess the efficiency and effectiveness

with which inputs are used to achieve intended outputs, and *evaluation* activities, which assess the extent to which projects or programs have achieved their intended objectives and have produced their intended changes and benefits in the target populations. In other cases the term *evaluation* is used more broadly to cover both of these functions. [Bamberger, 2000, p. 96]

Schaumburg-Müller (1996) defines ECB more broadly:

A broad definition of the concept of evaluation capacity building has been applied to the donor survey. It includes activities, which provide support for systems of evaluation, audit, feedback, and learning from policies, programs, or projects performed at various levels, mainly in the public sector. Although the concept is defined broadly, it excludes activities aimed solely at planning and appraisal activities. Also, the interest focuses on activities, which are not just of a temporary nature but have the aim of supporting a sustainable evaluation function. Therefore, support for temporary monitoring and evaluation units connected with a specific aid activity is excluded unless it provides evaluation training of a more general and sustainable nature to host-country staff. [p. 5]

In a similarly broad way, Boyle, Lemaire, and Rist (1999) define evaluation capacity development as follows:

Evaluation regime refers to the configuration of evaluation capacity, evaluation practice, organizational arrangements, and institutionalization. *Evaluation capacity development* refers to activities and initiatives taken to implement the regime. [p. 6]

Also broad is Mackay's (1999) definition of ECD as "the development of national or sectoral evaluation systems" (p. 2). Picciotto (1998) is even more expansive, defining it as "the ability of public institutions to manage information, assess program performance, and respond flexibly to new demands" (p. 39).

These definitions can be placed alongside our conceptual and working definitions. Both emphasize the common theme that ECB is about the development of a sustainable evaluation effort that can be located on levels from a local to an international level. These expansive definitions of ECB hold many promises for good government, rational decision making, and accountable performance.

ECB Promise. Throughout the literature, a number of statements have been made about the promise of ECB. It was seen by Schaumburg-Müller (1996) as good governance and as promoting efficient public management. Mackay (1999) reported that ECD is "an important aid to sound governance" and "a means to help achieve high levels of public sector performance" (p. 2). The promise for ECB was in the following four areas:

> First, evaluation findings can be an important input to government resource allocation (planning, decision making, and prioritization), particularly in the budget process.
>
> Second, evaluation assists government managers by revealing the performance of ongoing activities at the sector, program, or project levels—it is therefore a management tool that leads to learning and improvement in the future (results-based management).
>
> Third, evaluation findings are an input to accountability mechanisms—so that managers can be held accountable for the performance of the activities which they manage, and so that governments can be held accountable for performance . . .
>
> A fourth use of evaluation findings is in demonstrating the extent to which development activities have been successful. [Mackay, 1999, p. 2]

Hauge (1998) sees the promise of ECB as a way to help people reach goals, as an important cog in a nation's system of checks and balances, as a path to improved decision making, and as a process for utility for all levels of government. He pays particular attention to the systemic quality of ECB—that it is a system of action that is used to influence other systems so as to create a new system in which evaluation and its uses are regular, everyday practices. More specifically, Hauge sees the promise of ECB in helping to improve management of all resources, not just aid resources; he sees it giving focus to development priorities, attracting more resources, and possibly reducing the workload of administering and evaluating donor aid funds.

Although the scope of ECB is international, government on all levels in the United States, national and local foundations, and other giving organizations such as United Way also can be understood as aid donors, making immediately relevant lessons learned from the international community.

What Has Been Learned About ECB?

Although ECB has been written about as having great promise, authors have also lamented that its potential has not been realized. Picciotto (1998) writes:

> At the outset, let me note a basic paradox. Considerable effort by scores of development assistance agencies over several decades has produced little in the way of evaluation capacity. The central objective of ECD—the creation of resilient evaluation organizations in developing countries that are capable of playing a significant role in resource allocation and policy formation—has proven elusive. [p. 39]

Authors have identified a number of factors that have contributed to ECB, not fully realizing its promise as a role structure and process—factors that were consistent with our own efforts to build evaluation capacity within small and large institutions in domestic public, private, and not-for-profit sectors; they appear in the four case studies. The difficulty in realizing ongoing ECB is surely a fertile area for research. Particularly fascinating may be the search for the contribution of evaluators in fostering and deflecting a fully flourishing ECB.

Lesson One: ECB Requires a Broad Stakeholder Base. The first lesson is that *the stakeholder base must be broad to create and sustain ECB.* The ECB literature says that to reach a point at which quality evaluation and its appropriate use are ordinary and ongoing practices, ECB practitioners must pay attention to all relevant systems and players as stakeholders.

Bamberger (2000), Schaumburg-Müller (1996), and Hauge (1998) all found that the promise of ECB often was mitigated by an overemphasis on the needs and interests of donors, to the exclusion of other stakeholder groups:

> In many developing countries, donor agencies continue to be the main sponsors of evaluation. Consequently, donors' information priorities and evaluation methodologies continue to exert considerable influence on how evaluation is practiced and used. [Bamberger, 2000, p. 96]

> The evaluation of development projects and programs in developing countries has been dominated by donors, with almost each national and multilateral aid agency having established an evaluation unit with its own agenda. [Schaumburg-Müller, 1996, p. 4]

A concern is that in the ECB efforts so far, other stakeholders' voices, in particular the individuals affected by the development programs, are not taken into consideration. Bamberger (2000) writes: "There is increased concern about giving voice to the poor and other groups affected by development programs and policies" (p. 97).

Hauge (1998) reports that United Nations Development Programme (UNDP) mandates are putting greater emphasis on creating and sustaining systems of participation and inclusiveness for aid beneficiaries. As such, ECB must include both these ongoing structures and individuals. Further, it is necessary to meet the social and moral value that evaluation as an intentional process must be transparent:

> UNDP's mandate and programming objective is sustainable human development (SHD). The people-centeredness of the SHD concepts entails a philosophical belief in participation—as a means, but also as an end in its own right. Accordingly, UNDP also believes in an evaluation model that puts emphasis on participation and inclusiveness. However, in addition to our perception of participation as a substantive developmental priority, we believe

there is evidence that insisting on inclusiveness and openness is an imperative functional approach to ECD.

Poor people should be entitled to a voice in determining whether a poverty program is a success. It is better to have an imperfect answer from someone who has a legitimate claim to concern than a perfect answer from an expert whose mind is elsewhere. Among program stakeholders, special concern is needed for the representation of the ultimate intended beneficiaries.

Similarly, the process of evaluation planning and conduct needs transparency. Respect for the function is dependent on being able to understand what purpose evaluation is to serve; what criteria were applied in determining subjects of evaluation, in selecting evaluators, and in choosing the methodologies applied. Trust in the function is undermined when evaluation is conducted "inside a black box." [pp. 28–29]

There is no simple solution or even agreement on the moral imperative of beneficiary participation, as the literature in the United States over the past thirty years has shown (Fetterman, Kaftarian, and Wandersman, 1996; Baizerman and Compton, 1992; Stockdill, Duhon-Sells, Olson, and Patton, 1992; Whitmore, 2000). These issues are particularly acute when there are great discrepancies in social power, income, and education, and when the ideal is a viable and authentic involvement in a democratic process.

As external and internal evaluators, we too have found that donor needs (whether the donor is the federal government, a foundation, or United Way) often take precedence over the needs of other stakeholders. Yet the Joint Committee's standards stipulate in the *Stakeholder Identification Standard* that we must all make sure that "persons involved in or affected by the evaluation should be identified, so that their needs can be addressed" (p. 25). Often missing from practice may be the evaluator's obligation to attend also to the wants of persons who are affected by evaluation. This latter phrase serves to see the other person more as a political being than as a client.

In sum, this section has shown how ECB does not work unless it is recognized as an inherently political process. Power, authority, goals, coalitions, and the rest require a more or less well known and understood political base to give the work social and political legitimacy. These points from international ECB work are easily brought to our own organizations with their internal and external constituencies and where evaluations of education and human service agencies and programs engage these same concerns.

Lesson Two: ECB Requires Broad-Based Demand. Effective ECB requires broad-based demand. Demand is used typically as the source for both evaluation and ECB and also as a goal (that is, the creation of demand that leads to evaluation and to ECB). This is one perspective on how stakeholders are "identified" or "produced."

The ultimate test of the effectiveness of an evaluation system and thus also of ECB assistance is whether it is being used effectively in a sustained manner and contributing to decision-making processes at the level for which the system is designed. Unless there is a demand and use of the evaluation results, sustainability will not be achieved. [Schaumburg-Müller, 1996, p. 7]

Once again the work of the Joint Committee's standards can be linked to ECB via the notion of demand. As evaluators, we are asked to make sure that evaluations "address pertinent questions" and are "responsive to needs and interests of clients and other stakeholders" (Joint Committee on Standards for Education Evaluation, 1994, p. 37). Does this not mean that we should pay attention to "demand"? This is one perspective on how stakeholders are identified. From the political point of view, both demand and stakeholders are not just identified but are actively produced as partners in the process. Clearly, the ECB process must begin at this early stage of locating and naming demand and stakeholders. Our conceptual definition begins with the creation of processes rather than at the point where one takes on the management of already ongoing activities. The econometric model of demand in some ECB literature is here made social, then political, thus making explicit the moral basis of this practice. For us, as is clear in our conceptual and working definitions, "sustainability" can never be achieved once and for all. Hence, we use the word *sustentation* in the spirit of an infinite game, open-ended and ongoing (Carse, 1986).

Lesson Three: Demand and Purpose Must Be Matched. Effective ECB needs to match demand and purpose. Many ECB authors have used the words *accountability* and *learning* or saw the promise of ECB as being used as an accountability or learning tool (Schaumburg-Müller, 1996; Mackay, 1999; Hauge, 1998; Horton, 2001; Lee, 1999). From the evaluation practitioner's and ECB points of view, we have often seen the push-pull tension between evaluation purposes for accountability or learning. Although administrators or funders may state that they believe in organizational learning, the way evaluations sometimes are used is as a win-lose, "gotcha" game. Horton (2001), for example, found much resistance to ECB because of negative experiences in the past in which external, accountability-focused evaluations led to "sometimes . . . dramatic unexpected results, such as the closure of the program being evaluated or the firing of program staff members" (p. 2). It wasn't until ECB began to recognize the importance of local demand, use participatory approaches, and expand the evaluation purpose to improve the program that individuals "became eager to participate in it" (p. 3).

ECB, therefore, is most effective when there is alignment between the source and type of demand and purpose of the evaluation. This requires clarity among multiple stakeholders at the beginning and throughout both the evaluation and ECB process regarding whether the purpose of the evaluation is for accountability, program improvement and learning, or a combination of both. In order for this to occur, the process must be transparent and negotiated. The Joint Committee's standards on values identification require evaluators to make explicit "perspectives, procedures, and rationale to be used to interpret the findings" (Joint Committee on Standards for Education Evaluation, 1994, p. 43). This means that clarity of purpose (one of the utility standards) is of utmost importance because it serves to link demand and purpose in the overall ECB process, as well as for each discrete study.

Recognized as a political process of shifting coalitions, this point about evaluation demand and purpose reemphasizes ECB as a political process within the context of organizations and communities.

The point is that successful ECB needs a genuine foundation of purpose and clients. Demand is not a construct or conceptual logic but a result of practical need—the existence of people who actually want to make sure of an evaluation function for some rational purpose (Hague, 1998).

Lesson Four: ECB Operates on Many Levels. ECB works at identifying and integrating multiple-level, multiple-system evaluation activities. One of the important lessons from the international ECB is moving the evaluation view beyond the program level to the larger organizational levels. In practice, it appears that earlier international ECB efforts, although recognizing all the various levels involved when trying to build evaluation capacity within a country, have fallen short in part because not all levels have been considered. For example, Schaumburg-Müller (1996) found:

> Many developing countries have several evaluation systems operating at various levels: (a) at the national level, for instance attached to the planning process; (b) at the ministry or department level where a monitoring and evaluation unit is responsible to senior management; and (c) at programme or project level. Particularly at the programme and project level, the establishment of [monitoring and evaluation] M&E units is often donor-driven and financed. Although there are different evaluation needs at the various levels, an uncoordinated system risks wasting resources and creates confusion as regards the purpose and use of evaluation.

Hague (1998) makes a similar point in his reference to "clear roles and linkages," which are required when "building on the unique national institutional environment." Taken together, these points about national governments and ministries fit also for agencies, programs, and communities. As shown in the case studies, the CDC and the ACS are both nationwide in scope, with multiple sites and multiple levels within and across sites and ECB efforts to identify and then link appropriately the varieties of evaluation practice.

Lesson Five: ECB Requires Many Methods. Effective ECB requires a wide variety of evaluation approaches and methodologies. Stufflebeam (2001) describes several acceptable evaluation approaches. ECB literature pushes the perspective that such a wide range of approaches and related methodologies is necessary if evaluation is to be adopted as a routine, everyday practice in international work. The point is also made by Mackay in his case study on the World Bank and is clear in the ACS and CDC case studies.

Lesson Six: ECB Lacks Resources. The promise of ECB is limited by the lack of necessary financial and human resources. Because ECB is an intentional ongoing process, a wide variety of human and fiscal resources is required. Creating tension within ECB is a typical absence of long-term commitment to sufficient and timely allocation of resources. Clearly, in many international contexts the human resource skills necessary for quality evaluation practice and sophisticated ECB work are missing.

This point is made by almost all authors of international ECB literature (Boyle and Lemaire, 1999; Boyle, 1999; Schaumberg-Müller, 1996) and in the case studies, particularly in reference to organizational funding priorities, actual allocations, and staff turnover.

The issue of resources is highly contested across all organizations and especially so when in reference to the evaluation activity and when evaluation studies are linked to funding. This complex set of relationships between ECB, discrete evaluations, and resources appears throughout everyday ECB work and must be understood as issues of both political economy and of organizational priorities.

It is crucial for ECB work at all levels that resources be understood as more than evaluation knowledge and skills. The term *resource* also refers to the capability of facilitating and managing the ECB process. Some roles that have been identified by a long-time ECB practitioner who is also a case author are the

- Champion role (often at a senior level within an organization)
- Manager or coordinator of ECB activities (which has elements of salesmanship and advocacy and could include organizing others to conduct evaluations, provide evaluation training, or provide evaluation advice
- Technical evaluation functions

In a small organization, all these roles might be combined into one, but in a larger organization there would likely be a team of people with somewhat specialized role expertise. Remembering that ECB work is different from evaluation work, it is expected that the role repertoire of the ECB practitioner will be broad and fit the organizational context—structure and culture—which is basic to effective ECB practice.

Lesson Seven: ECB Must Be Flexible. ECB requires attention and crafting for multiple contexts. Because ECB is profoundly contextual in terms of the structure, culture, resources, politics, and ideologies of the organization, program, or other site, any effort to bring in a "canned" ECB structure or process is likely to fail, particularly in the long run. This is precisely because the ECB process is ongoing and open, and requires continuous adjustments and refinements.

ECB efforts, at times, have taken the form of ready-made systems developed by evaluation experts and superimposed on national and local efforts. This was not effective. Schaumburg-Müller (1996) concludes:

> An uncritical transfer of ready-made evaluation systems has few chances of being adopted and used. The design and formulation of evaluation functions have to be tailor-made for the circumstances of the individual country and organization. While there might be common objectives at a general level, the specific institutional, political, and management systems and approaches do need to be considered. A sustainable strategy has therefore to be built on host country decision-makers' and managers' needs and on the specific institutional and administrative circumstances under which the system has to operate. At the same time, new systems must also be seen in a reform context and provide performance and learning incentives for the public sector. [p. 18]

ECB practice is context-dependent and as such requires acute attentiveness to site, structure, culture, and everyday ways of working. One cannot decide a priori what is likely to be the most effective ECB strategy or way of working in the same sense that quality evaluation practice demands crafting each study to meet demand and purpose. Just as Stufflebeam (2001) calls on evaluation practitioners to be knowledgeable in a variety of approaches and related methods, the ECB literature calls on its practitioners to be similarly well versed in a large repertoire of ECB processes and practices. As internal and external evaluators, have we ever become so enmeshed in our own "models" that we have not truly considered the local context and the extent to which our approaches are appropriate? Stufflebeam's review calls on us all to critically examine our practice and determine the extent to which it matches up with the Joint Committee's standards. In his conclusion, he calls for trainers providing for their students "instruction and field experience in these approaches. When students fully understand the approaches and gain relevant, practical experience, they will be in a position to discern which approaches work best under which sets of circumstances" (p. 91).

To many practitioners, it is easier to understand culture when the reference is international ECB work, but, as we all know, culture is a very useful concept for understanding our profession, as well as the organizations and programs and other sites in which we work. Both quality evaluation and quality ECB work must be culturally responsive and responsible.

Conclusion

Our major points regarding ECB are as follows:

- ECB and evaluation practice differ.

- Whether our work is international or local, in small or large organizations, as internal or external evaluators or as ECB practitioners, the international ECB literature has much to teach.
- ECB cannot be understood as other than context-dependent, intentional work in organizations. The nature of these contexts is basic to quality ECB practice and theory, whether as art, craft, or science.
- ECB is a legitimate, important professional practice in its own right.
- No particular number of discrete evaluation studies brings about an organization's ECB process.
- The ECB perspective can be taken on by evaluators and others to enrich their own practice.
- Little is known about what it takes to successfully sustain the ECB process.
- Typically, evaluation work is done within a range of accepted conceptual frameworks, approaches, and methodologies; this range must be expanded and enriched to maximize evaluation's contribution to ECB.
- ECB itself must be subject to evaluation, and a meta-evaluation must be done of discrete ECB studies; what is learned from the evaluation of ECB and the meta-evaluation must inform the practice of program evaluation and the practice of ECB.

A Reading Frame

Chapters Two, Three, Four, and Five each present a case study of ECB practice, written following common guidelines to allow for comparison. In Chapter Six, a summary and analysis of themes across cases is provided.

Recall that ECB is a context-dependent, intentional action system of guided processes and practices for bringing about and sustaining a state of affairs in which quality program evaluation and its appropriate uses are ordinary and ongoing practices within and/or between one or more organizations/programs/sites.

As you read each case study, use the following elements to guide your reflection. How does the ECB work? Is it

Context dependent?
Showing the building and sustaining of intentional action systems?
Shown to be guided by the practitioner?
An overall ECB process?
Showing actual ECB practices?
An example of bringing about a "state of affairs" in which evaluations are completed and put to use?
Bringing about a "state of affairs" which makes possible evaluation studies and their uses?
Accomplished within and/or between organizations, programs, and other sites?

Built on quality program evaluation?

Showing the appropriate uses of quality program evaluation?

Showing the ordinary practices which constitute ECB in that organization?

References

Baizerman, M., and Compton, D. *From Respondent and Informant to Consultant and Participant: The Evolution of a State Agency Policy Evaluation.* New Directions for Program Evaluation, no. 53. San Francisco: Jossey-Bass, 1992.

Bamberger, M. "The Evaluation of International Development Programs: A View from the Front." *American Journal of Evaluation,* 2000, *21*(1), 95–102.

Boyle, R. "Professionalizing the Evaluation Function: Human Resource Development and the Building of Evaluation Capacity." In R. Boyle and D. Lemaire (eds.), *Building Effective Evaluation Capacity: Lessons from Practice.* New Brunswick, N.J: Transaction Publishers, 1999.

Boyle, R., and Lemaire, D. (eds.). *Building Effective Evaluation Capacity: Lessons from Practice.* New Brunswick, N.J.: Transaction Publishers, 1999.

Boyle, R., Lemaire, D., and Rist, R. C. "Introduction: Building Evaluation Capacity." In R. Boyle and D. Lemaire (eds.), *Building Effective Evaluation Capacity: Lessons from Practice.* New Brunswick, N.J.: Transaction Publishers, 1999.

Carse, J. *Finite and Infinite Games.* New York: Ballantine Books, 1986.

Fetterman, D. M., Kaftarian, S. J., and Wandersman, A. *Empowerment Evaluation: Knowledge and Tools for Self-Assessment & Accountability.* Thousand Oaks, Calif.: Sage, 1996.

Hauge, A. O. "Evaluation Capacity Development: Lessons Learned by the UNDP." In African Development Bank and World Bank, *Evaluation Capacity Development in Africa: Selected Proceedings from a Seminar in Abidjan.* Washington, D.C.: World Bank, 1998.

Horton, D. "Evaluation of Capacity . . . Capacity for Evaluation." From International Service for National Agricultural Research (ISNAR). Guest contribution, 2001. [Online at capacity.org/2/editorial.html]

Joint Committee on Standards for Education Evaluation. *The Program Evaluation Standards* (2nd ed.). Thousand Oaks, Calif.: Sage, 1994.

Lee, Y. "Evaluation Coverage." In R. Boyle and D. Lemaire (eds.), *Building Effective Evaluation Capacity: Lessons From Practice.* New Brunswick, N.J.: Transaction Publishers, 1999.

Mackay, K. "A Diagnostic Guide and Action Framework." *Evaluation Capacity Development* (ECD Working Paper Series No. 6). Washington, D.C.: World Bank, 1999.

Olds, L. E. *Metaphors of Interrelatedness.* Albany, N.Y.: State University of New York Press, 1992.

Patton, M. Q. *Utilization-Focused Evaluation: The New Century Text.* (3rd ed.) Thousand Oaks, Calif.: Sage, 1997.

Picciotto, R. "Evaluation Capacity Development: Issues and Challenges." In African Development Bank and World Bank, *Evaluation Capacity Development in Africa: Selected Proceedings from a Seminar In Abidjan.* Washington, D.C.: African Development Bank and the World Bank, 1998.

Schaumburg-Müller, H. "Evaluating Capacity Building: Donor Support and Experiences." Report for the DAC (Development Assistance Committee) Expert Group on Aid Evaluation, OECD (Organization for Economic Cooperation and Development). Copenhagen, Denmark: DANIDA (Danish International Development Assistance), 1996.

Stockdill, S. J., Duhon-Sells, R. M., Olson, R., and Patton, M. Q. *Voices in the Design and Evaluation of a Multicultural Education Program: A Developmental Approach.* New Directions for Program Evaluation, no. 53. San Francisco: Jossey-Bass, 1992.

Stufflebeam, D. L. *Evaluation Models.* New Directions for Evaluation, no. 89. San Francisco: Jossey-Bass, 2001.

Whitmore, E. (ed.). *Understanding and Practicing Participatory Evaluation.* New Directions for Evaluation, no. 85. San Francisco: Jossey-Bass, 2000.

Stacey Hueftle Stockdill is founder and CEO of EnSearch, Inc., a specialized evaluation firm in St. Paul, Minnesota.

Michael Baizerman is a professor in the School of Social Work and adjunct professor in the College of Education and Human Development and in the School of Public Health at the University of Minnesota, St. Paul.

Donald W. Compton is director of the Division Evaluation Services, American Cancer Society, National Home Office, Atlanta.

2

This chapter summarizes efforts to strengthen program evaluation capacity at the Centers for Disease Control and Prevention (CDC). We review the circumstances that triggered an interest in building this capacity in public health, along with the principles and procedures used by the working group charged to achieve this goal.

Building Capacity for Program Evaluation at the Centers for Disease Control and Prevention

Bobby Milstein, Thomas J. Chapel, Scott F. Wetterhall, David A. Cotton

Program evaluation is one of ten essential public health services (Public Health Functions Steering Committee, 1994) and a critical organizational practice in public health (Dyal, 1995). Until recently, there has been little agreement among public health officials on the principles and procedures for conducting such studies. In 1999, the CDC published *Framework for Program Evaluation in Public Health*, which specifies steps and standards for evaluating public health programs. The framework defined effective program evaluation as "a systematic way to improve and account for public health actions by involving procedures that are useful, feasible, ethical, and accurate" (Centers for Disease Control and Prevention, 1999, p. 1). This definition emphasizes prominent uses for evaluation (improvement and accountability) while acknowledging the need for adhering to a set of practical standards that make routine evaluations possible. The CDC views the

Many people have been vocal champions in the ongoing effort to strengthen the CDC's capacity for program evaluation. Space limitations prohibit us from naming everyone who has served in this capacity, but the most influential have included Jeffrey Koplan, Martha Katz, Claire Broome, Virginia Bales, Steve Thacker, Kathy Cahill, Jim Marks, Janet Collins, Marshall Kreuter, Dixie Snider, and Nancy Cheal. We also acknowledge and thank the other members of the CDC Evaluation Working Group, as well as the many contributors and consultants who so generously shared their perspectives with us in the hope of improving the effectiveness of the CDC and other public health organizations.

framework as "both a synthesis of existing evaluation practices and standard for further improvement" (Centers for Disease Control and Prevention, 1999, p. 34).

The CDC engages in a vast array of evaluation activities and has several well-developed evaluation systems.[1] Even so, its distribution of evaluation expertise is uneven; in general, evaluation is "not practiced consistently across program areas, nor is it sufficiently well-integrated into the day-to-day management of most programs" (Centers for Disease Control and Prevention, 1999, p. 1). As the nation's prevention agency, the CDC is obliged to continually strengthen its capacity for program evaluation so that it accounts for its stewardship of public funds and can shape programs and policies that are effective in improving health.

From 1997 to 2000, the CDC undertook a concerted effort to elevate the importance of program evaluation at the agency and to strengthen its capacity for conducting such studies. This chapter examines (1) why strengthening evaluation capacity became an explicit priority at the CDC, (2) what the principles and procedures for building that capacity were, (3) what the effects of capacity-building activities have been, and (4) some lessons learned while doing this work within a federal public health agency. Readers will benefit from understanding the CDC's experience because within this case study are examples of five basic elements that have been proposed as a general framework for building evaluation capacity: motivational forces, organizational environment, workforce and professional development, resources and supports, and learning from experience (Milstein and Cotton, 2000).

Context for Building Evaluation Capacity at the CDC

The CDC is widely regarded as the world's premiere scientific institution for promoting population health and preventing disease, injury, and premature death. With an annual budget of approximately $2.8 billion, the CDC encompasses 13 centers, institutes, and offices and employs approximately 8,500 persons in 170 occupations. Employees are housed in 10 CDC facilities, as well as in state and local health agencies, quarantine offices, and other countries. Born as the Malaria Control in War Areas unit within the U.S. Public Health Service, the CDC adopted its famous acronym in 1946 when it became known as the Communicable Disease Center (Etheridge, 1992). Since then, its name has changed three times to keep up with expanding efforts in areas such as environmental health, occupational safety and health, injury prevention, and chronic disease prevention. By the time the words *and Prevention* were added to *Centers for Disease Control* in 1992, the CDC had been positioned as "the nation's prevention agency" and adopted as its vision, "healthy people in a healthy world through prevention" (U.S. Department of Health and Human Services, 2001).

The expansion of the CDC's name and mission mirrors larger changes throughout the sphere of public health. In the last half of the twentieth century, public health organizations made significant strides controlling infectious diseases, only to see chronic diseases become the major causes of morbidity and mortality throughout the industrialized world. The control of chronic diseases (as well as injury, HIV-AIDS, and other emerging health concerns) is a daunting challenge, in part because individuals must change their behavior and those changes must be sustained for a lifetime. Furthermore, accumulating evidence on health disparities has revealed that many health problems are tied to larger community conditions and systems, which themselves have to be transformed to make significant progress toward improving community health. For organizations like the CDC, the need to affect community and systems factors in addition to individual health behaviors has demanded that new sciences be brought to bear, new expertise be integrated into the workforce, new partners be engaged, and new relationships to those partners be established.

By the mid-1980s, a concern for addressing the social determinants of health added further force to a widespread reappraisal of the very purpose of the public health agency. Among the groups and institutions that have considered this issue, the Institute of Medicine, through its landmark monograph *The Future of Public Health* (Institute of Medicine, 1988), has probably been the most influential. This monograph encouraged public health officials to organize their work around three core functions (assessment, policy development, and assurance) rather than continue to deliver direct services to those at risk for disease (as had been the norm in many instances). Making the transition to a "new" form of public health practice that embraces the core functions has had profound implications for CDC programs, as well as for the agency's overall evaluation strategy.

In 1993, the Government Performance and Results Act (GPRA) (Government Performance and Results Act, 1993) was passed into federal law amidst a nationwide trend toward increasing the accountability of the public sector. GPRA required federal agencies to create an annual performance plan, define tangible performance measures, and monitor annual progress on those measures. The CDC's fulfillment of the law's requirements led to a resurgence of attention across the agency to strategic planning and evaluation while simultaneously serving as a reminder of just how much capacity is needed for the typical program to routinely document and evaluate the results of its efforts.

The notion of accountability is particularly complex when applied to CDC programs, which are usually funded through three- to five-year cooperative agreements with health departments, universities, community-based organizations, national voluntary associations, and other partners. Approximately three-quarters of the agency's overall budget is allocated to grantees under such mechanisms, with each given considerable autonomy in focusing their efforts and evaluating their work. This decentralized structure presented unique challenges when Congress and other stakeholders began asking, through GPRA requirements and other inquiries, what federal agencies had achieved with their funding (General Accounting Office, 1998). Their legitimate questions about performance highlighted how difficult it is to document and attribute health effects to specific interventions, especially when broader demographic, economic, and social forces also affect health status.

With demands for accountability and results at a high level, the CDC faced the problem that many of its programs involved collaborative, multifaceted initiatives with communities around the nation and the world. Engaging these community partners demanded complex approaches melding policy, structural, and individual change that were (1) implemented differently in different contexts and (2) hard to measure feasibly and consistently. Furthermore, the ultimate outcomes of interest, such as reductions in hypertension, HIV infection, obesity, or violence, were ones that might take years to materialize. The CDC remained committed to showing that its efforts as an agency were worthwhile. Yet understanding the precise effects of a single program under these circumstances proved to be an extraordinary challenge.

The changing character of public health, coupled with ongoing organizational changes within the CDC, created a receptive environment for the idea of building evaluation capacity. During a 1997 leadership retreat, the agency got the spark it needed to work on the issue. Two senior staff members lamented the CDC's inability to practice evaluation in a consistent manner, also questioning how decisions were made about which programs to evaluate, when, how, and by whom. The other senior staff, including the CDC director, regarded these weaknesses in capacity for program evaluation as significant gaps in the agency's overall capability—ones worthy of immediate attention.

A short-term study group of eighteen senior staff met four times over the next several months. The group's final report concluded that the CDC needed to enhance its evaluation capacity by developing a working definition of *evaluation,* formulating an evaluation framework, creating a focal point for leadership on evaluation within the organization, building an evaluation-literate workforce, nurturing a culture of accountability, and sharing evaluation information across the agency (Centers for Disease Control, 1997). A new group, the CDC Evaluation Working Group, was then formed to examine these recommendations in greater detail and begin the process of building evaluation capacity both within the CDC and throughout the public health system.[2]

Building Evaluation Capacity

A concern for building evaluation capacity at the CDC is not new. The agency first established an Office of Program Planning and Evaluation back in 1972 and has since had an evaluation officer coordinating the CDC's evaluation activities. In addition, a competitive process for funding program evaluations has existed since the early 1970s, and centrally administered support contracts have been in place since 1988 to facilitate access to external contractors with evaluation expertise.

Concerns about whether the CDC as a whole benefits fully from evaluation science are not new. Study groups in the 1970s looked at this issue, and reports in 1991 (Research Triangle Institute, 1991) and 1997 (Battelle Center for Public Health Research and Evaluation, 1997) examined how CDC program evaluations were conducted and proposed ways to improve them. Even so, the evaluation function tended to develop in an idiosyncratic and fragmented fashion across the agency. Because each public health program was engaged with a different set of issues and its own partners, approaches to evaluation grew increasingly diverse. Some groups sponsored full-scale evaluations, whereas others did little systematic evaluation at all. Formal requests for proposals, applications, and contracts invariably required an evaluation plan, but these tended to portray evaluation as an afterthought, seemingly apart from the main workplan. Evaluation tasks were often delegated to subcontractors and divorced from the responsibilities of senior project staff. As a result, CDC project officers and grantees did not routinely engage in full, ongoing discussion about what should be evaluated and how those evaluations should be conducted. These and other historical factors set the stage for the newly formed working group that got under way in 1997.

Operating under the auspices of the CDC director,[3] the working group was charged with defining both the science base and organizational role for program evaluation in public health. This charge offered the opportunity to promote a greater shared understanding of what evaluation science is and how it can be used to improve public health policies and programs. The charge also called for an examination of the CDC's internal culture, as well as the agency's place within the larger sphere of public health.

Members and Contributors. Participation in the working group was open to all interested parties. Each center, institute, or office designated one lead representative, and other staff were encouraged to participate as fully as they wished. Diversity was an important asset for the group, especially in some program areas such as infectious disease, chronic disease, injury; academic background, experience with evaluation, and organizational role (for example, program, research, policy) were also diversified. Throughout the group's deliberations, it had approximately 25 active members; an additional 250 persons eventually became involved as consultants or contributors as a result of the group's effort to engage various sectors of the public health workforce both inside and outside the agency.[4]

Interpreting the Charge. The CDC's senior leaders understood that strengthening evaluation capacity in public health would require a process of culture change, including significant reforms to their own organization. They asserted that the CDC should build an evaluation-literate workforce and maintain a cadre of applied evaluation scientists throughout the agency.

These goals, they explained, could be accomplished only partly through training in evaluation, with additional strategies focusing on leadership and other aspects of organizational infrastructure (Centers for Disease Control and Prevention, 1997).

The willingness of agency leaders to embark on a course of institutional change was shared by managers and staff throughout the organization, greatly enhancing the prospects for success. Although the working group was asked to provide several specific products, such as a working definition of *evaluation* and mechanisms for information exchange, it also had an unequivocal charge to begin the process of transforming the CDC's institutional culture into one more conscious of the need for evaluation and more engaged in practicing it routinely.

The first task the group faced was to translate the broad charge into an easily understandable operational strategy that would motivate a large number of diverse stakeholders. The aim was to generate useful, highly visible products for stakeholders both inside and outside the organization. Two specific written products were proposed: (1) a framework for program evaluation in public health, to be published in the CDC's most visible venue for scientific policy, the *MMWR Recommendations and Reports* series, and (2) recommendations to promote program evaluation practice at the CDC, with options for implementation, to be submitted to the CDC director and senior staff of each center, institute, or office.

Time Frame. The time line of significant events and activities for the working group is presented in Figure 2.1, with the two major products shown as diamonds. The group's Web site quickly became a consistent and cumulative focal point for the effort, allowing those who were interested to participate and remain up to speed, even if they could not attend meetings. The time between September 1997 and February 1998 was reserved for listening to contributor input and reviewing relevant literature. Draft versions of the two written products, which began circulating early in the process (October 1997), provided a stimulus for contributor input, conversation, and problem solving. The Workshop to Develop a Framework for Program Evaluation in Public Health (February 1998) convened stakeholders, organized the information already collected, and helped to align elements of the emerging framework and strategic plan.

After the workshop, the group focused on confirming the work they had produced, with six months devoted to consolidating and vetting recommendations (March–August 1998) and nearly a year and a half (March 1998–September 1999) engaged in field testing and refining the framework. A nationwide satellite training program in October 1998 used elements of the framework for its curriculum and exposed almost ten thousand participants to the group's ideas. One year after the initial recommendations were presented, the group held a follow-up meeting with several senior staff to reflect on accomplishments and discuss next steps. Also, just two months

Figure 2.1. Events and Activities, CDC Evaluation Working Group: 1997–2000

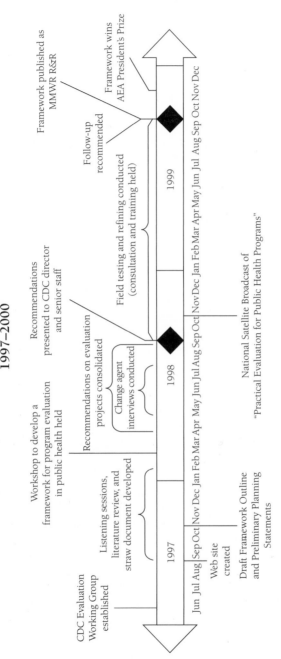

after its publication in November 1999, the framework was awarded the President's Prize at the annual meeting of the American Evaluation Association (AEA).

Principles, Processes, and Procedures. Several principles guided the working group in its deliberations—principles that made explicit its assumptions about which strategies might be effective in strengthening the CDC's capacity to conduct sound evaluations, given its unique organizational climate. These principles asserted that (1) evaluation is best conducted at the program level and integrated into program operations; (2) agencywide coordination is essential; (3) adequate resources are needed to conduct sound evaluations; (4) greater capacity is needed for internal evaluation at all organizational levels; (5) support is needed for state, local, and community partners to participate in evaluation; and (6) leadership, incentives, and long-term culture change are necessary at the CDC and throughout the public health system.

Within the working group, evaluation was understood to be an inherently volatile subject that raises concern about deeply held values and the power dynamics of who decides what is best and how such conclusions are reached. The group's willingness to adopt and maintain a transparent, open stance toward the subject soothed much of the anxiety associated with the prospect of more extensive evaluation. The neutrality and trustworthiness conveyed by the group's processes effectively turned potential critics into contributors and, in many cases, allies. Without such broad-based support, the eventual products (the published framework and recommendations for institutional change) would most likely not have been as well received.

Finally, iterative information-sharing procedures were used for developing each of the desired products. These included "listening sessions," literature review, development of draft documents, field testing, and dissemination and adaptation. The sections to follow summarize the major observations from each.

Listening Sessions. The working group spent over five months engaged in listening sessions, which were designed to find out what public health workers understood about evaluation and how they viewed its role in improving public health effectiveness. Approximately two hundred CDC staff and fifty representatives from other organizations participated, either individually or in groups, with a variety of formats ("brown-bag" discussions, individual interviews, group interviews, workshops). On nine occasions, entire organizational units (for example, branches or divisions) came together to talk about evaluation. Regardless of format, there were always two lines of discussion: one on views toward evaluation, the other on strategies for institutional change.

Among the take-home messages from these conversations were seven "opportunities for culture change" that were expressed as recurring themes:

1. A common language and greater understanding of the many meanings of evaluation is essential, particularly because the public health

workforce is multidisciplinary and thus lacks a shared educational background.

2. Program goals and expectations could be communicated more clearly through the routine use of program logic models; once developed, those models could serve as templates for data-collection systems to monitor critical indicators along the presumed pathways of change.

3. Much could be done to increase confidence in the methods of evaluation science and to use a more diverse set of methods in evaluation projects. For instance, many analytic techniques in the social and behavioral sciences had yet to be acknowledged by opinion leaders within the CDC as legitimate, particularly quasi-experimental designs and certain qualitative methods.

4. CDC staff ought to model good evaluation practice through self-scrutiny (for example, by evaluating their own role in a collaborative program). External partners might better appreciate the importance of evaluation if they saw their CDC counterparts engaging in evaluation activities of their own.

5. Internal capacities for evaluation could be enhanced through new directions in leadership, funding, recruitment, training, technical assistance, and information sharing.

6. Honesty in evaluation is impossible to achieve within an environment of threat, resistance, and mistrust. It would help to reframe the fear of "failure" by promoting the notion that "learning programs" make up a "learning organization."

7. Ultimately, an evaluation perspective bridges gaps between researchers, program practitioners, and policymakers—all of whom must work together better for the collective culture to change around evaluation.

Contributors in the listening sessions also pointed out close connections between the task of building evaluation capacity and other "cross-cutting trends" affecting the public health system. Six trends in particular were identified as widespread and having strong ties to evaluation capacity. These included (1) *community involvement,* which mandates that public health activities be planned, implemented, and evaluated with the full participation of affected stakeholders; (2) *health information systems integration,* which attempts to link disjointed sources of information about population health; (3) *workforce and infrastructure development,* which strives to enhance both the human and organizational resources of public health agencies; (4) *accountability to Congress and other constituents,* which reminds all public sector employees of their ultimate responsibility to demonstrate how their work serves the public interest; (5) *prevention research,* which answers questions about the efficacy of interventions and the strength of causal models; and (6) *evidence-based practice,* which encourages public health workers always to seek out and enact scientifically sound programs and policies.

The effort to integrate program evaluation into routine public health practice was indeed closely tied to these trends and to several others. Seeing these connections reinforced our understanding of the need for institutional change within the CDC and added a deeper level of significance to the group's charge. By listening to contributors, the working group came to see that the movement to build capacity for evaluation could not proceed as an isolated initiative. Instead we had to study the forces of change affecting other aspects of public health and devise strategies for supporting evaluation practice that would also align with those concurrent changes. Failure to make those connections might have led to the evaluation function being overlaid on "real" public health work instead of tightly integrated with it.

Literature Review. An exhaustive review of the evaluation literature was neither feasible nor necessary because the group was seeking a practical working understanding of evaluation. Trying to balance large principles at the core of evaluation philosophy with the specific activities that evaluators perform in their daily practice, group members examined published and unpublished materials, Web sites, conference proceedings, and the AEA electronic discussion forum "EVALTALK." They looked for ways of organizing evaluation concepts into specific actions that might connect directly to routine CDC program operations, and they kept an eye out for information about evaluation practice standards that might guide practitioners in making (or assessing) inevitable trade-offs regarding an evaluation's design, conduct, or use.

A frequent problem was contending with the complex ways in which evaluation is discussed in the professional literature. Dealing with the proliferation of terms and synonyms and wrangling with the semantic distinctions made by authors throughout the field fostered misunderstanding among those who approached public health work from differing points of view. The absence of a unifying conceptual framework made certain aspects of evaluation appear to be sharp dichotomies (for example, impact versus outcome, outcome versus process, formative versus summative, improvement versus accountability, performance measurement versus evaluation) when, in our experience, the differences were not always clear-cut (for example, one partner's process is equivalent to another's outcome) and not as important as identifying the fundamental attributes that all evaluation projects share. Thus the group saw the need for their framework to be a broad, practical, nonprescriptive guide that public health professionals could use when planning, conducting, or reading about an evaluation project. The framework eventually created (Centers for Disease Control and Prevention, 1999) had just two dimensions: (1) steps in evaluation practice, which synthesized information about what evaluators actually do, and (2) standards for effective evaluation, which endorsed in their entirety the program evaluation standards put forth by the Joint Committee on Standards for Educational Evaluation (1994).

The search for written resources had at least two benefits beyond providing a firm grounding in scholarship of the field. First, it put the group in contact with a diverse network of persons and organizations doing innovative evaluation work. Second, it allowed us to compile a set of resources for conducting evaluations, many of which were available electronically and could be disseminated readily through the group's Web site.

Development of Draft Documents. An indication of the group's seriousness is that, just days after their first meeting, members circulated draft versions of documents that were precursors to the two written products they had been asked to develop: (1) an outline of critical elements to include in the framework for program evaluation and (2) a set of recommendations to enhance the role of evaluation practice at the CDC and beyond. Both drafts were quite specific, effectively circumventing what might have been a protracted discussion about evaluation philosophy and forcing group members to decide precisely what things were important for them to say and do.

The draft framework began with a short list of key points, which rapidly expanded to a seventeen-page annotated outline that incorporated just about everyone's favorite issue. Each week, as new information was incorporated from the ongoing listening sessions and literature review, members discussed the organization of concepts and their appropriate level of emphasis. With strong, yet fair, facilitation, this process eventually brought the group to a practical consensus about what the framework should contain.

The recommendations for institutional change at CDC evolved differently. Working group staff were vigilant about recording each contributor's suggestions for what could be done to enhance evaluation capacity at the CDC and throughout the sphere of public health. Even the most informal suggestions were noted. The group also kept a running log of take-home messages from every listening session, document, or field-test experience. These notes accumulated over seven months (September 1997 through March 1998), yielding approximately two hundred specific observations and recommendations. To consolidate this material, we developed a systematic process for sorting, rating, and clustering each item. Part of the job involved reviewing the entire set of recommendations to ensure that they were balanced with regard to those that would promote the will (or the desire) to initiate evaluations, the means (or the resources) to enact them, and the knowledge (or the understanding) necessary to meet or exceed the standards for sound evaluation. The result was a set of twelve recommendations—six directed at the program level (the CDC's organizational units responsible for program and policy initiatives) and six directed at the CDC as a whole (the agency level); see Table 2.1.

With these recommendations in hand, the working group consulted with sixteen "change agents" from across the agency. Taking this step acknowledged that different groups within the CDC would differ in their

Table 2.1. Recommendations to Promote Program Evaluation at the CDC

Program Level	Agency Level
Designate Coordinators and Staff Designate an evaluation coordinator for each major program with appropriate expertise to lead evaluation and program improvement efforts. Assign FTEs and hire qualified staff to collaborate in evaluation practice at the program level.	*Designate an Organizational Lead or Champion* Designate an organizational entity to be the agencywide focal point and champion for evaluation and program improvement.
Dedicate Resources Allocate funds (beyond those awarded from the 1 percent program) for evaluation and program improvement.	*Develop an Evaluation Consultation Corps (E-Corps)* Establish a neutral "Evaluation Consultation Corps" to help CDC staff and partners conduct evaluation.
Create Logic Models with Linked *Evaluation Plans and Information Systems* Develop program-specific logic models with corresponding evaluation plans and information systems.	*Coordinate Policies and Activities* Streamline existing activities and policies to ensure that the agency has a coherent and cohesive approach to evaluation and program operation.
Conduct Evaluations Initiate focused evaluations to assess and improve program plans, operations, or effects.	*Train Staff* Increase the evaluation literacy of the CDC workforce and provide tailored educational opportunities for staff to learn about their role in evaluation practice.
Create Technical Assistance Directories Create a directory of resources for evaluation technical assistance in each program area to help partners in state, local, and community organizations.	*Produce Materials* Produce and disseminate user-friendly materials to support evaluation practice and to share findings from evaluations of public health programs.
Create Incentives Create incentives, maintain leadership visibility, and reward achievement in evaluation practice. Reduce obstacles to evaluation practice and use.	*Sustain Leadership* Maintain leadership visibility to promote the importance of evaluation in public health practice. Encourage inquiry and foster a results-based program improvement orientation.

strengths and the challenges they faced in building evaluation capacity. The group tried to offer recommendations that responded as closely as possible to those differences in organizational climate and stage of readiness to practice evaluation. The main goals for seeking feedback from change agents were to clarify perceived advantages, disadvantages, and implications of potential recommendations; better understand specific organizational factors that might help or hinder progress toward institutional change; elicit new ideas and creative combinations of recommendations; and enlist the support of opinion leaders to increase the chances that recommendations would eventually be enacted. By vetting proposed recommendations with persons in each center, institute, or office, the group was able to understand more about their perceived merit and feasibility and the degree of commitment in place for alternative strategies to promote evaluation capacity. As a consequence, recommendations went forward with the unanimous consent of all working group members.

Field Testing. An unanticipated but vital part of the working group's activities involved field testing (March 1998 through September 1999) the program evaluation framework. There had always been an intention to do some reality checking before publishing a framework, but no one could have foreseen the intense interest that existed within the CDC (and beyond) for consultation and training on program evaluation.[5]

Requests for ad hoc consultation came in slowly at first, then accelerated. By the end of August 1998, fourteen consultations had taken place; by December another twenty-eight had begun; and after a year and a half the total completed exceeded eighty-six, reflecting increasing prominence and awareness of the group, as well as the expanding interest in evaluation throughout the field. Each interaction was approached as a new opportunity to understand how public health professionals confront evaluation issues in their work. Behind the scenes, staff constantly revised the framework, thereby increasing its utility. Without the involvement and trust of so many practitioners, the framework that was eventually published would not have been so well refined nor so widely accepted.

Dissemination and Adaptation. The group combined efforts to disseminate the framework with ongoing support for those interested in incorporating its principles into their work. In the first three months after publication, nearly 62,630 copies of the framework were distributed, either electronically or by mail (Milstein, Wetterhall, and others, 2000). These reports were distributed worldwide, with greater concentration among persons and organizations throughout the U.S. public health system, often moving through naturally occurring networks such as groups of program collaborators or staff of entire organizational units.

Circulation was relatively rapid in government and university settings, but interest developed more slowly among community organizations in public health. To reach this important audience, the CDC worked with the Center for the Advancement of Community-Based Public Health to produce an adapted version designed to explain evaluation to community leaders and engage them in evaluation activities as stakeholders and full partners (Baker and others, 2000). Approximately two thousand copies of this adapted version have been disseminated.[6]

Both the originally published framework and its adapted version were intended to be general, encouraging readers to use each "as a template to create or enhance program-specific evaluation guidelines" (Centers for Disease Control and Prevention, 1999, p. 35). Many practitioners have accepted this invitation and report that the framework is indeed helpful for various tasks.[7] Two examples of the many adaptations we know about are the CDC's *Updated Guidelines for Evaluating Surveillance Systems* (Centers for Disease Control and Prevention, 2001a) and the national tobacco control program's *Introduction to Evaluation, Planning, Implementation, and Use* (Centers for Disease Control and Prevention, 2001b). From the standpoint of building evaluation capacity, these and other adaptations represent significant accomplishments in making evaluation practice an integral part of program operations within the CDC.

Assessing Efforts to Build Evaluation Capacity

The most significant accomplishment of the CDC Evaluation Working Group was its affirmation that building capacity for evaluation never ends. Through its products and processes, the group emphasized ways in which all public health workers can engage in evaluation practice and thereby expand their organization's capacity to do so. By listening to stakeholders and examining the role of evaluation under various circumstances, we found that the ability to evaluate programs routinely also entails ongoing work, on an institutional level, to establish the conditions under which evaluation can occur and prosper.[8] This challenging task has no logical end, nor can it be fulfilled by just one person or group at one place or time. Instead, capacity building must proceed through activities that are self-perpetuating. By this standard, the working group was successful. One example is its creation of the framework, which has been replicated on multiple levels by multiple programs. Another is its decision to recommend institutional changes at both the program and agency levels, knowing that even partial progress in either area would stimulate change in the other.

Within a relatively brief time, the working group succeeded in becoming a visible catalyst for change. Its framework was not only accepted by CDC opinion leaders but also adopted as agency policy and awarded high praise by evaluation professionals. Many of the terms and concepts introduced by the group have shaped how staff talk about evaluation among themselves and, more significantly, with their partners. Training courses on evaluation have been revised to correspond with the framework, and groups not previously exposed to such training have enrolled in high numbers. Requests for ad hoc consultation have continued to accrue (both from organizational units within the CDC and as partner organizations), and the CDC is now regarded as an important source of information and expertise on program evaluation, as it is in scientific areas like epidemiology. Moreover, the working group's inclusive process helped identify persons with special interest in evaluation as an important but previously unrecognized constituency. Finally, a senior health scientist was appointed to the Office of the Director, with responsibility for continuing to build evaluation capacity both within the CDC and throughout the public health system. In these ways, the self-perpetuation required for building evaluation capacity continues.

These developments add to a long history at CDC of efforts to strengthen evaluation capacity in public health generally. Initiatives dating back to the 1970s, which remain in place today, laid the foundation for critical evaluation functions such as setting measurable objectives (for example, the "Healthy People Objectives") and establishing permanent data-collection systems for health status (for example, the National Health Interview Survey) and health behavior (for example, the Behavioral Risk Factor Surveillance System). The CDC Evaluation Working Group did not try to reinvent or rebuild existing infrastructures. Instead it sought to clarify the nature of current evaluation practice and position it organizationally as something to which everyone could contribute. Moreover, its work can be seen as just the first of a three-phase effort; the focus on the CDC's internal capacity for evaluation was the first step. The second task might be to support capacity building among partner organizations; and the final step would help the entire public health system engage in collaborative evaluation based on a shared concern for mutual accountability and a desire to improve community health.

Accomplishments of the working group support the conclusion that it was successful in strengthening the CDC's evaluation capacity, but no systematic assessments of this work have been performed. One problem is that the evaluation profession as a whole still lacks a well-developed theory and associated indicators for understanding evaluation capacity at an organizational level, particularly its inherent change over time and "ongoingness." Still, such an assessment would be consistent with the goal of continually building capacity, and thus it is a step that the CDC and its partners ought to take.

Additional steps have been proposed for perpetuating the effort to strengthen evaluation capacity at the CDC that address each of the five dimensions outlined in the AEA presidential strand on building evaluation capacity (Milstein and Cotton, 2000). They include accentuating links between evaluation, planning, and budgeting (motivational forces); formally celebrating program innovations and successes (also motivational forces); making evaluation a consistent focus in the CDC director's annual program review (organizational environment); customizing training to the needs of specific audiences and programs (workforce and professional development); creating opportunities for mentoring on evaluation (workforce and professional development); enhancing tools for self-guidance (resources and supports); developing outlets for presenting evaluation case studies, reporting findings, and reflecting on lessons learned (learning from experience); and enacting previous recommendations that have not been fully implemented.

Lessons Learned

The most profound lesson we learned about building evaluation capacity was also the most straightforward: people and organizations learn evaluation by doing it. No amount of education or exhortation fully prepares one for the task. Above all else, reflective experience is the key to acquiring the capacity for sound evaluations. In this regard, the program evaluation standards (Joint Committee on Standards for Educational Evaluation, 1994) are essential. Most public health professionals are constantly evaluating their work, if only informally, but they may benefit greatly by using the standards to question whether a given set of evaluative activities are in fact sound and working to their potential. Even without other interventions, raising awareness about the standards can lead to increased evaluation capacity and better evaluation practice.

If experience doing evaluation inherently builds capacity, then fear and misperception, which prevent projects from getting under way in the first place, stand as the greatest obstacles to progress. Common concerns about evaluation must be addressed and predictable lines of defense countered to overcome the inertia associated with beginning new evaluation projects.

In our experience, three chief lines of defense are raised against evaluation: resources, righteousness, and resistance. Resources for evaluation are unquestionably important, but even projects with limited means can conduct sound evaluations. Moreover, well-funded ventures face many of the same conceptual challenges as poorly funded ones in accomplishing certain evaluation tasks (engaging stakeholders, defining the program, posing questions, negotiating standards for success). The second defense pertains to righteous attitudes, which assume that a program works in the absence of evidence. These views can be countered by inviting advocates to document their successes and thereby help others replicate proven accomplishments. Finally, psychological resistance (the third defense) stems from the human instinct to avoid criticism, judgment, and change. Such concerns are legitimate, but they can be alleviated by emphasizing learning instead of punishment, program performance instead of employee appraisal, and adaptation instead of stability.

The perception of a punitive environment is antithetical to sound evaluation practice. To build capacity, agency leaders must convince staff and stakeholders that answering evaluation questions thoroughly and honestly is more important than getting results that look and feel good. Thus, within the CDC, we are exploring ways of rewarding programs not only for documenting success but for using "negative" findings to make substantive changes in their approach.

Finally, we have learned to remain mindful that gains in evaluation capacity are fragile. Apparent progress is always vulnerable to staff turnover, setbacks, and other kinds of disruption. Obstacles both large and small stand in the way of changing to a stronger evaluation culture. Even with commitment and will, change will most likely be gradual. A progressive transition that gains strength and expands over time is therefore the most realistic expectation. In this context, leaders must be agile and take advantage of "teachable moments" (for example, new initiatives or reorganizations). Most organizations, including the CDC, have a way of remembering how early adopters of innovations, like evaluation, are treated. Thus opinion leaders must be selective about which projects they take on and supportive of new approaches when the program environment changes. They must also understand organizational culture and monitor forces of change beyond their own agency's walls. Knowing the organization's culture is perhaps the most valuable asset for those seeking to create an evaluation-friendly environment.

Reflections of the Definition of Evaluation Capacity Building

The conceptual definition put forward by the editors of this issue outlines a vision of evaluation capacity that we also sought to achieve in our work at the CDC. It defines a state of affairs in which evaluation is a routine and respected organizational practice. Precisely how this state of affairs is created and sustained remains an area for further exploration. An essential first step is the compilation of case studies, such as those in this volume and others yet to be told. As we review these case examples, however, an important distinction might have to be made between the conditions that confer evaluation capacity to an organization and the strategies used to bring about those conditions and sustain them over time. The former is a theoretical question, the latter an empirical and practical one. Regardless of how these issues are sorted out, it seems clear that in the future, advocates for enhanced evaluation practice must also speak out for building evaluation capacity. In our experience, the two are inseparable.

Summary

To strengthen evaluation practice in public health requires more than understanding its methods, collaborating with evaluation experts, hiring evaluation contractors, or creating new teams, branches, and divisions on organizational charts. Although these changes may occur, a deeper shift in the culture and mind-set is needed throughout the sphere of public health for evaluation practice to prosper. Leaders of public health agencies and of grassroots organizations will have to work in complementary ways to bring about an evaluation culture in public health (Trochim, 2001; Sanders, 1993). Many scholars have said and we have now come to understand that although evaluation uses the methods of science it entails much more than that. Evaluation's special role is to draw together and connect processes that are usually fragmented in organizations, such as planning, research, action, infrastructure building, policy setting, marketing, decision making, and leadership. To confine evaluation to one of these categories undermines its role and weakens its potential contribution.

The CDC's official policy on program evaluation concludes by saying, "Public health professionals can no longer question whether to evaluate their programs; instead, the appropriate questions are: What is the best way to evaluate? What is being learned from the evaluation? And, How will lessons learned from evaluations be used to make public health efforts more effective and accountable?" (Centers for Disease Control and Prevention, 1999, p. xx). If we begin to answer these questions honestly, then improvements in evaluation capacity are sure to follow.

Resources

Documents described in this report are available electronically through the CDC Evaluation Working Group Web site: cdc.gov/eval/index.htm. For additional information, send an electronic message to the working group at eval@cdc.gov.

Notes

1. Programs such those sponsored by the Division of Adolescent and School Health, the Office on Smoking and Health, and the Division of HIV/AIDS Prevention have exceptionally strong evaluation systems.

2. Two of the authors (Wetterhall and Milstein) were assigned to work full-time on the evaluation working group. Chapel and Cotton served as contributors but at the time were not employed by the CDC. Our review is therefore a synthesis of these internal and external perspectives on the working group's activities.

3. The CDC Evaluation Working Group operated under the auspices of the Office of the Director, Office of Program Planning and Evaluation. The group's genesis among senior staff and organizational placement in the Office of the Director conferred a high degree of management visibility on the effort.

4. Participation was sought from eight sectors of the public health workforce: evaluation experts, public health program managers and staff, state and local public health officials, nonfederal public health program directors, public health organization representatives and teachers, community-based researchers, U.S. Public Health Service agency representatives, and CDC staff.

5. The working group did not actively seek out consultation opportunities. Instead they made it known that if others were willing to talk about evaluation endeavors, group members were willing to listen.

6. "An Evaluation Framework for Community Health Programs" can be accessed via the Internet at cdc.gov/eval/evalcbph.pdf.

7. Reported uses for the framework include writing funding proposals; clarifying program strategies; guiding specific evaluation projects; developing guidelines, policies, and practices for evaluation; training public health professionals and students; and creating complementary resources for supporting evaluation activities. For additional details see Milstein, Wetterhall, and others, 2000.

8. Factors that enable evaluation to prosper are trusting partnerships, clear program plans, norms for questioning and reflection, systems for gathering credible information, negotiated standards for success, and, most important, assurance that lessons learned will be used for improvement, not punishment.

References

Baker, Q. E., Danis, D. A., Gallerani, R., Sanchez, V., and Viadro, C. *An Evaluation Framework for Community Health Programs.* Durham, N.C.: Center for Advancement of Community-Based Public Health, June 2000.

Battelle Center for Public Health Research and Evaluation. *Assessment of the Programmatic Impact of One-percent Evaluation Studies.* Arlington, Va.: Battelle, 1997.

Centers for Disease Control and Prevention. *Evaluation at CDC Study Group Report.* Atlanta: Office of Program Planning and Evaluation, 1997.

Centers for Disease Control and Prevention. "Framework for Program Evaluation in Public Health." *Morbidity and Mortality Weekly Report,* 1999, *48*(RR-11), 1–40.

Centers for Disease Control and Prevention. "Updated Guidelines for Evaluating Surveillance Systems." *Morbidity and Mortality Weekly Report,* 2001a, *50*(RR-13), 1–35.

Centers for Disease Control and Prevention. *National Tobacco Control Program: An Introduction to Evaluation Planning, Implementation, and Use.* Atlanta: Office on Smoking and Health, National Center for Chronic Disease Prevention and Health Promotion, 2001b.

Dyal, W. W. "Ten Organizational Practices of Public Health: A Historical Perspective." *American Journal of Preventive Medicine,* 1995, *11*(6), Suppl 2, 6–8.

Etheridge, E. W. *Sentinel for Health: A History of the Centers for Disease Control.* Berkeley, Calif.: University of California Press, 1992.

General Accounting Office. *Managing for Results: Measuring Program Results That Are under Limited Federal Control.* GAO/GGD-99–16. Washington, D.C.: General Accounting Office, 1998.

Government Performance and Results Act of 1993. Public Law 103–62. August 3, 1993.

Joint Committee on Standards for Educational Evaluation. *Program Evaluation Standards: How to Assess Evaluations of Educational Programs.* (2nd ed.) Thousand Oaks, Calif.: Sage, 1994.

Institute of Medicine. *The Future of Public Health.* Washington, D.C.: National Academy Press, 1988.

Milstein, B., and Cotton, D. *Defining Concepts for the Presidential Strand on Building Evaluation Capacity.* American Evaluation Association. Available at eval.org/eval2000/public /presstrand.pdf

Milstein, B., Wetterhall, S. F., and the CDC Evaluation Working Group. "A Framework Featuring Steps and Standards for Program Evaluation." *Health Promotion Practice,* 2000, *1*(3), 221–228.

Public Health Functions Steering Committee. *Public Health in America.* Washington, D.C.: U.S. Department of Health and Human Services, 1994. Available at health.gov/phfunctions /public.htm

Research Triangle Institute. *Final Report: Development of CDC Evaluation Strategy.* Research Triangle Park, N.C.: Research Triangle Institute, 1991.

Sanders, J. R. "Uses of Evaluation as a Means Toward Organizational Effectiveness." In

S. T. Gray (ed.), *Leadership IS: A Vision of Evaluation. A Report of Learnings from Independent Sector's Work on Evaluation.* Washington, D.C.: INDEPENDENT SECTOR, 1993.

Trochim, W.M.K. "An Evaluation Culture" In *Research Methods Knowledge Base* [on-line textbook, 2nd ed, 2001.] Available at trochim.human.cornell.edu/kb/evalcult.htm

U.S. Department of Health and Human Services. *CDC Fact Book 2000/2001.* Atlanta: Centers for Disease Control and Prevention, 2001.

BOBBY MILSTEIN *is evaluation coordinator, Centers for Disease Control and Prevention, Division of Adult and Community Health, Atlanta.*

THOMAS J. CHAPEL *is senior health scientist, Centers for Disease Control and Prevention, Office of Program Planning and Evaluation, Atlanta.*

SCOTT F. WETTERHALL *is director, Health Assessment and Promotion, Dekalb Health Department, Decatur, Georgia.*

DAVID A. COTTON *is vice president, ORC Macro, Atlanta.*

3

This story from the American Cancer Society (ACS) describes how its first evaluation practitioner came to do ECB because of the need for evaluation following changes in the organizational structure. A short history of these changes is described as background for understanding the seven ECB principles used at the ACS.

Ongoing Capacity Building in the American Cancer Society (ACS) 1995–2001

Donald W. Compton, Rebecca Glover-Kudon,
Iris E. Smith, Mary Eden Avery

This chapter tells the story of ongoing ECB efforts within the ACS. It is written from the point of view of the practitioners who began this work in 1995 and continue it to the present. We present the challenges facing them as they oriented their practice toward making evaluation and its uses routine and essential to the organization's work, including its goal setting, decision making, program planning, and everyday management. Although the story is specific to the ACS, experience suggests that the issues are similar to those facing ECB practitioners in other organizational settings.

The authors regard ECB as an intentional action system whose processes are designed to achieve broader and deeper evaluation and the better use of evaluation. At the ACS, ECB processes can be described as having three aims: (1) developing and sustaining an evaluation unit, (2) creating organizational capacity to conduct and use evaluations, and (3) developing the organizational structure and other supports necessary for promoting and using evaluation processes and results.

To tell the story of ECB at the ACS, six topics are addressed:

1. The organizational and larger context of ECB in the ACS
2. The history of ECB at the ACS
3. Practice principles used to develop and sustain ECB in the ACS
4. How the practice principles have been operationalized
5. How we assess ECB in the ACS
6. The lessons we learned

NEW DIRECTIONS FOR EVALUATION, no. 93, Spring 2002   © Wiley Periodicals, Inc.

47

The central focus of our ECB work is increasing the ability of the ACS to achieve its broad goal of controlling cancer. To best understand our ECB, the organizational and larger context of our work must be described because both have a considerable influence on what we do and how we go about it.

The Organizational and Larger Context

A fundamental understanding of the ACS as an organizational context is crucial to understanding how we approached ECB. Between 1995 and 2001, this context was fluid and complex, with frequently changing organizational forms, practices, and roles for staff and volunteers—all of which was strongly influenced by the larger social context. It is necessary to understand both the organizational and the social contexts in order to see how ECB was designed and carried out and how it continues to be carried out.

The Organizational Context. The ACS is an eighty-seven-year-old, nationwide, community-based, volunteer organization with little history of formal evaluation prior to the opening of its first evaluation unit in 1995. The mission statement for the ACS states that it is "dedicated to eliminating cancer as a major health problem by preventing cancer, saving lives, and diminishing suffering from cancer through research, education, advocacy, and service" (American Cancer Society, 2000). This overall mission is linked to a broad goal of cancer control and to more specific "challenge goals" that include reducing age-adjusted cancer incidence rates by 25 percent and age-adjusted cancer mortality rates by 50 percent by the year 2015. ACS funds come primarily from individual donations and corporate philanthropy. There are an estimated 2 million volunteers, 7,000 staff, and $477 million allocated for program services. The organizational structure of ACS comprises a national home office (NHO), 17 regional offices (divisions), and approximately 3,400 community-level units (American Cancer Society, 2001).

Between 1997 and 2000, a nationwide reorganization resulted in the merger of fifty-seven state-level offices into seventeen strategically focused regional offices. This restructuring was intended to eliminate duplication of services and to provide each regional office with sufficient resources for its major work of reducing the burden of cancer on patients and their families. Although each regional office is an independent entity, each is "chartered" by the NHO in a document that makes explicit how the national and regional office will work together to accomplish common goals.

Within regional offices, there is variation in how staff and volunteers serve their local community. Some regional offices retain a unit structure made up of volunteers from small and large communities and supported by staff from regional or local offices. Other regional offices organize staff and volunteers across the region to work together on a specific cancer site, such as the breast or the prostate. These differences are important to ECB. The strength of the ACS, regardless of its local organizational structure, is its ability to implement programs locally and advocate for cancer patients and their families.

A second set of major organizational changes was the 1996 reduction in size of the national board of directors from 225 to 43 voting members, and their adoption of a policy governance model that made them responsible for setting and monitoring the organization's overall goals and policies. Responsibility for operational decisions was given to the CEO at the NHO. Two levels of accountability were thus made explicit and linked to outcomes. Part of the reason for these changes was a shift in where and how the program development process takes place; related directly to this were complementary changes in the role and power of staff and volunteers in program creation.

A second result was to integrate evaluation demand into the program development process; a third was to locate one type of demand in a particularly important department—Cancer Control. These shifts in the internal organization of the ACS had dramatic consequences for the new evaluation unit, and these effects continue.

Prior to these organizational changes, volunteers played a major role nationally and locally in determining which services were provided and in what ways. Now scientifically based programs are developed by NHO staff, pilot-tested, and diffused nationwide for local implementation. This change has been important for ECB because evaluation is now a regular and ongoing part of this program development process, particularly in the national Cancer Control Department.

This shift in program planning created both an opportunity and a challenge for the evaluation unit and its organizationwide ECB work because almost no ACS staff had knowledge about formal program evaluation. Thus the evaluation unit became a guide to the NHO and the field in its evaluation work across a range of ACS activities by facilitating national evaluation studies, providing regular training to staff and volunteers, synthesizing regional studies, and providing technical assistance and consultation to both the NHO and the field. In these ways, the ECB work was linked to the changing organizational structures and practices, at the same time the authors were building a responsive, professional evaluation unit. These changes in ACS structure and in the evaluation unit are best understood in the larger external context because it directly influenced how ECB was understood and carried out.

The Larger Context. Seven developments in the larger context help us understand how ECB developed evaluation work within the ACS. These include United Way of America's requirements for logic models and outcome measures; the demand for accountability from donors and other funding sources such as foundations; the national economy; increased competition for donor funds; increased overall acceptance of evaluation nationwide;

increased emphasis on internship requirements within schools of public health; and a movement by the ACS toward working more collaboratively with other organizations at both the national and local levels.

First, the ACS annually receives approximately $40 million from United Way offices nationwide. With the development of United Way requirements for program logic models and outcome measures, there is increased interest on the part of ACS staff and volunteers at both the national and regional levels to learn how to respond to these requirements. Previously, few ACS program staff used logic models to make program theory explicit. Now, however, logic models and "measurable goals" are institutionalized in the NHO program development process. This creates new opportunities for the evaluation unit's ECB work, including educating program staff about the benefits of evaluation and teaching evaluation approaches and methods as noted.

Second, most philanthropic and government grants, as well as the ACS's own donors, have increased interest in evaluation. All of this supports the ECB effort to co-create and co-sustain evaluation as a regular and routine process within the ACS.

Third, the growing economy has supported the development of greater evaluation capacity. The ACS program services budget grew from $397 million in 1999 to $477 million in 2000 (American Cancer Society, 2001), increasing the availability of funds both to initiate new cancer control efforts and to better support existing efforts. For example, Relay For Life, the ACS's signature fundraising event, involves over 1.5 million volunteers annually in over 2,700 events, bringing increased attention of communities to the question of whether the ACS spends its funds effectively, that is, accountability. This is heard, too, from funding sources, and there is greater interest by ACS leadership to demonstrate that they are responsible stewards of these funds. The increase in available funds at ACS has led to the hiring of more professionally trained staff who are knowledgeable in evaluation and better able to lead evaluation studies.

Fourth, more nonprofit organizations exist to prevent, control, and treat cancer. In 1990, there were 449 such organizations; in 1999, 686 competed with the ACS for donor funds (National Center for Charitable Statistics, 1990, 2000). This increase exerts external pressure on the ACS, bringing attention to fiscal accountability and stewardship, thus increasing the likelihood that evaluation will be linked to these demands and will become a regular and more highly valued activity throughout the organization. Evaluation has the potential to give the ACS a competitive advantage in the marketplace.

Fifth, the increased acceptance of evaluation nationwide has contributed to an ACS climate of greater openness to evaluation, and this grows as staff and volunteers realize the benefits of evaluation for providing accountability, demonstrating stewardship, and improving their programs and services—three reasons evaluation is needed.

Sixth, because of an increased emphasis on internship requirements, schools of public health became more open to collaborating with organizations to provide students with real-world work experience (Council on Education for Public Health, 1999).

Seventh, the ACS is part of the wider movement toward greater collaboration among organizations with shared interests, both nationally and locally.

The Story of ECB in the ACS

The ACS story begins with the hiring in 1995 of a new director of evaluation. The director was immediately caught in the tension between the need to conduct evaluation studies to meet existing demand and the fact that ECB was necessary for the longer-term sustaining and mainstreaming of evaluation. Meeting existing demand would require a large staff, for which no funds were allocated. This led to urgent discussions with a range of national and regional ACS staff and external professional evaluators about how best to proceed.

How could evaluation be conceptualized and carried out so that it would become a regular, ongoing practice within the organization? At first the task was conceived as prioritizing evaluation studies that would be strategically important to the organization. This strategy of showing the value of evaluation by evaluating three major ACS initiatives did not lead to the resources needed to build the evaluation unit nor to evaluation becoming a routine practice.

A second, more effective, strategy was to identify a pool of competent external professional contractors to meet the immediate evaluation demand. This was helpful but insufficient, in part because the ACS was reluctant to fund the cost of hiring professional contractors.

With internal and external advice and consultation, a deeper understanding of ECB and of the ACS was reached. It became clear that simply commissioning studies would not necessarily result in a broader and deeper use of evaluation work, nor in wiser and more focused requests for studies, nor in the penetration of evaluation into the ACS's higher policy and management levels. This recognition led to a larger conceptualization of how evaluation and its uses could contribute to organizational goals and to understanding what changes in organizational structure and culture might make the routine and ongoing use of evaluation processes and procedures more likely. This new overall concept is now called ECB. The CEFP was an effort in the larger ECB strategy.

CEFP as an ECB Strategy. CEFP, a collaborative effort between the ACS and schools of public health, is an ECB strategy for providing evaluation services to the ACS. CEFP was conceived through conversations with the associate dean for applied public health at Emory University's Rollins School of Public Health (RSPH), with advice from many others. These conversations revolved around how collaboration with RSPH and other universities could help to meet the ACS's need for practical and useful evaluation, while providing real-world evaluation training opportunities for graduate students. The associate dean's interest and expertise in evaluation and her understanding that students needed practical professional work experience led to envisioning collaboration. A pilot project began to test the ECB strategy at the NHO and in the field: Could low-cost, practical evaluation be done with students? The pilot revealed it could, and this early collaboration evolved into the ongoing program called CEFP.

The basic concept of CEFP is simple. It's the matching and integrating of complementary needs and resources. The ACS had limited evaluation resources to meet the ongoing demand for practical, useful, and timely evaluation; and schools of public health had large numbers of graduate students interested in real-world practical evaluation experience under faculty supervision. The ACS evaluation unit wanted to show ACS staff how evaluation could be helpful, and university faculty wanted to provide work opportunities. Funding from the Robert W. Woodruff Foundation allowed CEFP to be implemented nationwide in twenty-two universities. More than one hundred studies were completed during the project's first four years. A secondary benefit of CEFP was that outside funding facilitated ECB at ACS regional offices, in some local units, and at the NHO. For an overview of the CEFP, see Compton, Baizerman, Preskill, Rieker, and Miner (2001) and a special supplement of *Cancer Practice* (Preskill and Compton, 2001).

CEFP is one example of ECB to increase the organization's ability to conduct and use evaluation studies. The adoption of CEFP created a new demand for evaluation services; this, in turn, contributed to enlarging the evaluation unit. Through CEFP, both the field offices and the NHO learned about a model of practical and usable evaluation—Utilization-Focused Evaluation (Patton, 1997)—and an ACS-specific, fifteen-step evaluation process was crafted to meet the organizational structure, culture, and practices. By implementing relatively small studies, ACS staff and volunteers became more knowledgeable about participating in evaluation studies and using the results, while graduate students learned how to design, carry out, and report on evaluation studies. CEFP also created relationships with schools of public health that have been valuable for other purposes, including consultation for program development, for providing evaluation training to ACS by university faculty, and for facilitating studies by doctoral students.

However, CEFP is by itself insufficient to meet the ACS's current demand for larger-scale, longer, and more complex studies. The evaluation unit's four professional staff members provide consultation to the NHO and the field offices. These evaluation professionals manage studies and identify and nurture relationships with outside contractors. They also carry out regional training of ACS staff and volunteers. This is critical to increasing staff's knowledge, willingness, and skill in doing and using evaluation and in creating evaluation demand.

In combination, all of these human, fiscal, and ideational resources foster the growth and institutionalization of evaluation work. Taken together, all of this sustains and supports ACS's ability to meet the organizational demand for evaluation services. This demand, CEFP, and the growth in the evaluation department are all examples of the ACS's ECB work.

Practice Principles Used to Develop and Sustain ECB in ACS: Toward Lessons Learned

This section presents seven principles that have been used to increase the likelihood that evaluation will continue to be an essential practice within the ACS. The principles guide ECB work across the three structural elements of ECB: (1) overall process, (2) actual practices, and (3) occupational orientation and practitioner role.

1. *See with bifocals; focus on both the forest and the trees.* Focusing simultaneously on the forest and the trees, the near and far, the now and the future is the primary principle applied to all ECB work. In practice, this means to respond to the day-to-day organizational requests for evaluation services, while at the same time considering how the evaluation unit's response to this particular request may contribute to the unit itself and to evaluation practice becoming and continuing throughout the organization as a regular practice, that is, "the way things are done around here." This principle is a perspective on each study (that is, the tree), seeing it as enhancing the longer-term organizational change process of ECB (that is, the forest).

Focusing on the forest and the trees requires an ongoing, never-ending, and skillful reading of the organization, its players and their ways of working, and their ability to do and respond to all this continuously. Persistence and commitment to evaluation as a valued practice, to professional-level work, and to an openness to working in ways that fit ever-emergent situations are necessary.

2. *Adapt and operationalize a conceptual framework of evaluation and its uses within the Joint Committee Standards.* ACS adopted and adapted elements of the following into its working model of evaluation and its uses: the utilization-focused evaluation (UFE) philosophy (Patton, 1997) and the Joint Committee standards (Joint Committee on Standards for Education Evaluation, 1994) to enhance quality practical evaluation; the Preskill and Torres (1999) model for evaluative inquiry in organizations; and Himmelman's (1994) framework for collaboration.

These conceptual frameworks have provided ECB work with a common understanding of the purposes of evaluation, the evaluation process, the uses of evaluation, and an evaluation vocabulary. Staff and volunteers have followed these guidelines as they learned about the need for evaluations, how to budget for them, how to manage studies, and how to use the evaluation processes and products to improve their programs and to be accountable to clients, funders, and the ACS.

3. *Adopt strategies and tactics that are sensitive and responsive to the organization's structures, cultures, and everyday practices.* Throughout the ACS, decisions are typically made in a group process by staff and volunteers. As a form of participatory evaluation, UFE is compatible with this culture and has been put into practice through a fifteen-step process to meet this work norm. There are advisory group members for each study, and they are included during the evaluation process. The CEFP mirrors ACS organizational structure and culture by operating as a national project implemented at the local level, just as in the rest of the organization. In this way, the NHO evaluation unit supports the overall ECB-CEFP structure and processes, whereas the implementation of studies and their practical uses are controlled at the local level.

4. *Openly co-create and co-sustain evaluation through internal and external collaborations.* ECB is carried out collaboratively, with partners inside the ACS and outside: in universities, in the human services and education, and with evaluation firms and independent contractors. All partners are involved in setting objectives and getting the work done, as well as in evaluating and otherwise reflecting on the process. All work is done openly and responsively; without this way of working, co-creation and the long-term co-sustaining of evaluation capacity would be less likely. This "coworking," that is, constantly working collaboratively, also makes the work slower and transforms the work into the politics of coalitions and other small groupings.

5. *Be at all the tables that matter for ECB.* Participation in organizational decision making and planning is critical to making evaluation an essential and routine practice within an organization. If evaluation staff are not "at the table" when policy and program decisions are made, the evaluation function remains marginalized, decreasing the likelihood that it and its uses will become integrated into everyday organizational practices such as planning and program management.

6. *Evaluate the unit's work.* Evaluating the unit's own work means "walking the talk" and making sure this is known outside the unit. Through evaluating the unit's work, the routine use of evaluation is modeled for unit staff and outsiders. This can lead to more skillful work with other units within the organization, as well as to a more effective evaluation unit and thus to more effective ECB.

7. *Guide rather than control.* An orientation toward guidance rather than control is necessary in ECB. Most ECB work with others cannot be "controlled" by evaluation staff while they try to make co-creation and co-sustentation a transparent group effort (see principle 4). ECB practitioners can use this approach as part of a larger pedagogy in which they invite the organization to learn about and take on evaluation and its uses.

How the Practice Principles Have Been Operationalized

In order to make clear how we continue to work at ECB, this section shows how we simultaneously focus on both the forest and the trees. We will discuss the basics of ECB—developing the evaluation unit, creating organizational capacity to conduct evaluations, and moving the organization to use evaluation processes and products. We are working with the three ECB elements: the overall process, actual practices, and practitioner orientation and role.

Developing and Sustaining an Evaluation Unit. Developing and sustaining an evaluation unit can be a foundation for other ECB work. In its six-year history, the ACS's evaluation unit faced several critical moments—times when its very continuation was in question. These moments resulted from multiple reorganizations of the NHO and changes in three of the unit's supervisors. It was unclear at these times whether the unit would continue, how it fit in at the ACS, and its roles at the NHO and nationwide.

When the evaluation unit opened in 1995, it was the fruition of a vision by a national vice president for professional services. She envisioned how evaluation could contribute to cancer control through organizational development. In selecting a unit director, she wanted someone experienced in an internal evaluation unit, who had a vision of how evaluation could become a regular process, and who valued practice organizationwide over the longer term. That is, she held an unarticulated conception of ECB.

From the evaluation practitioner's perspective, developing and sustaining the evaluation unit focuses primarily on the finite task at hand, typically responding to the next request to conduct a study, standardizing data-collection instruments for use by multiple clients, and ensuring that evaluation products were used appropriately. In this view, developing and sustaining the unit was seen as responding to the demand for evaluation studies. Far less attention was given to the larger issue of systematically creating ways for evaluation to be seen as a regular practice throughout the organization.

For the ECB practitioner, however, which was the role soon to be taken by the new director of the evaluation unit, the focus shifted and was first on responding to requests for evaluation services while simultaneously considering how today's work will contribute to sustaining the unit in the longer term. This might be thought of as wearing bifocals, thus allowing a given situation to be assessed from two angles—one the angle of the program evaluation practitioner and the other angle of the ECB practitioner. In this case, the same person took both perspectives, shifting his awareness from one angle to the other. For example, in interactions with a client the program evaluation practitioner asks the question, "How will this contribute to making this a better study and make its uses more likely and make possible another quality study?" The ECB practitioner asks, "How will this moment in this particular evaluation contribute to the organization's learning and development such that a next study will be asked for and used?" In this way, the ECB practitioner considers how each study is connected to the organization's capacity to do and use evaluation studies and to achieving and sustaining a state of affairs in which this is done regularly and over time.

Later a third shift occurred. ECB became the main frame that evaluation studies and their uses fit within. At that point, the ACS had an ECB process, and the evaluation unit director was an ECB practitioner with an ECB orientation.

Each of the following examples of client interaction could be read through the evaluation practitioner or the ECB practitioner lens. Whereas the evaluation practitioner wants evaluation to become a regular practice throughout the organization, the ECB practitioner assumes responsibility for making this happen. The following examples highlight this concept.

Request for a Study by a Client Unfamiliar with Evaluation

- Evaluation practitioner's perspective: conduct the study.
- ECB practitioner's perspective: conduct the study while teaching the client evaluation terminology and an evaluation approach and process. The client will learn how to assume greater responsibility for evaluating the program in the future. This notion is consistent with the adage, "Give a man a fish and he eats for a day. Teach him to fish and he eats for a lifetime."

Addressing Joint Committee's Standards

- Evaluation practitioner's perspective: Use the Joint Committee's standards for guidance in conducting a study.
- ECB practitioner's perspective: teach about the evaluation profession through the application of the Joint Committee's standards so as to increase the perceived value of evaluation, including sensitizing the client to human subjects' requirements.

The ECB practitioner works to make evaluation and its uses regular organizational practices by working with his or her own staff and with other departments, clients, regional offices, and collaborating partners. Specifically, the practitioner participates in a range of professional activities, which includes receiving training in state-of-the-art ECB practice rather than evaluation practice. This means that the ECB practitioner is responsible for ensuring that "best practices" are used by evaluation practitioners. Directly related to best practices are the Joint Committee's standards.

The ECB practitioner must ensure that high-quality, practical, and useful evaluations are done in accordance with the Joint Committee's standards and are done in a timely way. It is the ECB practitioner's responsibility to ensure that the project itself contributes to how the client does the regular practice of evaluation now and in the future. The ECB practitioner matches the client's needs to the unit's strategies for sustaining the larger evaluation work. This is an important task because as demand for evaluation increases, clients become more able to assume some responsibility for using evaluation on a regular basis, needing less support from professional evaluation staff in the evaluation unit. In this way, evaluation practice is disseminated and adopted throughout the organization without increased resources. This makes the "selling" of the evaluation unit to clients easier and contributes to sustaining the unit.

Creating Capacity to Conduct Evaluations. An ongoing tension for most evaluation units is matching existing resources to the demand for evaluation services. Because no one strategy is sufficient to create the necessary type and amount of capacity needed to conduct a range of different types of evaluations, multiple approaches have been developed, adapted, and assessed over the six-year history of the evaluation unit. Early in this process, due to large demand and limited staff, it was clear that the evaluation staff alone could not and should not conduct evaluation studies; the unit would facilitate these evaluations. From a program evaluation practitioner's perspective, this means an ongoing search for external contractors to match the needs of specific studies.

In an ECB practitioner's perspective, creating capacity to conduct evaluations is seen as a way of creating linkages between each study and the larger overall organization's capacity to respond to evaluation demand over the longer term. For the ACS, the ECB approach was operationalized in several ways:

- Through CEFP, collaborations with universities were developed that provided a resource base of faculty within each of twenty-two universities with expertise in program evaluation (and related general public health and cancer-specific practices).
- This faculty group connects other university faculty doing regional studies to the NHO, which conducts nationwide studies. This group of evaluators also conducts training nationwide, provides consulting services on program development processes, and assists with synthesizing regional studies for use by the NHO.
- A resource pool of evaluators and evaluation companies complements the CEFP evaluators; they are used on a regular basis to conduct studies and provide technical support to the ACS's own evaluation work.

In these and other ways, the ECB practitioner defines the role of the evaluation department as a collaborating partner who faces inward toward the client's needs while facing outward to the overall organization and who provides technical expertise and support by systematically creating resources for the organization's evaluation needs and wants.

In combination, these strategies are important for ECB because they create ongoing, collaborative working relationships with a wide range of evaluators and organizations to meet the needs for evaluation services.

Developing the Capacity to Use Evaluation Processes and Products. In the past six years, this ECB component has received less attention than the first two. While the unit adopted a utilization-focused evaluation philosophy and developed its processes and procedures in accordance with UFE principles, fewer resources were devoted to internal ACS staff training because of demands on resources for creating and sustaining the evaluation unit and creating the capacity to conduct studies. However, with the maturation of the unit, training is now a primary work focus (for example, over the next three years in collaboration with RSPH and the CDC).

Training staff in using evaluation processes and products is made more difficult because there is no proven training pedagogy and the rate of staff turnover is high, both within CEFP (for example, evaluation facilitators) and throughout the ACS at all levels. This means, in effect, that there is always a relatively small base of ACS staff with training on even the basic level.

This aspect of ECB is under review at the ACS to determine the most effective strategy for enhancing the organization's use of evaluation through training and by using other strategies. However, as with other aspects of ECB work, no single strategy is sufficient to meet the varied demands, wants, and needs. Although this issue is under review, efforts have been devoted to laying a foundation for long-term collaboration with RSPH and the CDC to offer evaluation training to CDC and ACS staff.

For example, one result of these efforts was an ACS-CDC cosponsored training session in June 2001 for 150 CDC and ACS staff; the session was devoted to utilization competencies and application of the Joint Committee standards. This resulted from joint reflection on the state of evaluation at both the ACS and the CDC and the recognition that even with both agencies having evaluation units in place and the capacity to conduct quality evaluation studies, neither would make much progress without increasing staff competencies in using evaluation processes and products, within a better understanding of how the standards can be applied.

From the evaluation practitioner's perspective, developing the organization to use evaluation means working with individuals to use evaluation processes, such as creating logic models to make their program theory explicit, developing measurable objectives, and translating evaluation reports into action.

For the ECB practitioner, the focus is looking outward to other organizations as collaborative partners and inward to the ACS, realizing that the staff's use of evaluation processes and results requires a never-ending response due to staff turnover, changes in the state of the art, shifts in organizational goals, programs and procedures, and influences from outside the ACS, for example, in public health and biomedical science.

How We Assess ECB in ACS

Possibly the best indicator of the status of ECB in the ACS is found in recommendations from an evaluation work group convened by the chief operating officer in early 2001 to make suggestions for the future of the evaluation unit and its ECB work. This was, in effect, an assessment task. These NHO and field staff produced strong recommendations for expanding evaluation so it would contribute to all NHO departments and regional offices carrying out the ACS mission and meeting goals for the year 2015. They specifically recommended that ACS should (1) develop a strategy to increase understanding of the "business value" of evaluation; (2) achieve organizational consensus on utilization-focused evaluation and use of evaluation quality standards; (3) provide evaluation resources, consultation, and technical support to all levels of the organization; (4) design evaluations to inform decision makers about the impact of multi-tiered interventions, the effective allocation of resources, and strategies for course correction; (5) perform evaluation syntheses and identify "best practices"; (6) clarify appropriate roles for evaluation at various levels of the organization; (7) perform meta-analysis at the national level; and (8) expand its ability to formulate and conduct evaluation. In short, the group found that the evaluation unit was effective and that its mandate and mission should be expanded. Implicitly, they recommended an ECB role for the unit.

The evaluation unit regularly uses several formal and informal strategies to assess ECB. Overall, the unit follows up its studies to learn whether, once an evaluation report is disseminated, it is used; and how its intended users, among others, assess it. This follow-up work is now routine and thus is part of the ongoing ECB process. In addition, other, more formalized steps are taken to assess the uses of evaluation and customer satisfaction.

Assessment of ECB can begin with consideration of the current number of evaluation staff positions, demand for evaluation, and uses of evaluation in contrast to the past. Six years ago, there was little formal evaluation conducted at ACS; now evaluation processes have become routine practices within the organization. Regarding the number of staff with full- or part-time responsibility for evaluation, the NHO evaluation unit has grown from one to six. In the field, eight full-time staff and six part-time staff have responsibility for the evaluation function. At the NHO, demand for evaluation exceeds the capacity of the evaluation unit to respond.

Use of evaluation has been another focus of the evaluation unit's efforts to assess its ECB efforts. Over a two-year period, one case study examined evaluation use in seven regional offices, and another assessed CEFP evaluation reports (Mattessich, Compton, and Baizerman, 2001; Ritchie, 2001).

Missing from an evaluation of ECB efforts is an assessment of the development of user competencies among ACS staff and volunteers. As the ECB emphasis increasingly becomes the development of user competencies through regular training, this will become necessary.

Lessons Learned

The seven principles convey what has been learned about ECB over the past six years. A second summative point is that ECB is a family of dynamic processes, not an entity or thing; ECB work by its nature remains fluid, ever changing, and never complete. It is a world of multiple strategies, multiple processes, and multiple practices.

We have learned that the ECB process is identifiable in its outline and in some of its particulars and that ECB practices can be named, shown, and taught. Most clear is that the ECB occupational orientation to evaluation work such as this is grounded in the everyday practices of the four professional evaluators in the ACS evaluation unit. Together, they co-create and co-sustain evaluation capacity building at the ACS, both at the NHO and nationwide.

References

American Cancer Society. *Victory Within Our Reach: Annual Report 2000.* Atlanta: American Cancer Society, 2000.

Compton, D., Baizerman, M., Preskill, H., Rieker, P., and Miner, K. "Developing Evaluation Capacity While Improving Evaluation Training in Public Health: The American Cancer Society's Collaborative Evaluation Fellows Project." *Evaluation and Program Planning,* 2001, *24,* 33–40.

Council on Education for Public Health. *Accreditation Criteria: Graduate Schools of Public Health.* Washington, D.C.: Council on Education for Public Health, 1999.

Himmelman, A. "Collaboration for a Change: Definitions, Models, Roles, and a Guide to Collaborative Processes." In M. Herrman (ed.), *Resolving Conflict: Strategies for Local Government.* Washington, D.C.: International City/County Management Association, 1994.

Joint Committee on Standards for Education Evaluation. *The Standards for Program Evaluation.* Thousand Oaks, Calif.: Sage, 1994.

Mattessich, P., Compton, D., and Baizerman, M. "Evaluation Use and the CEFP: Lessons from a Case Study." *Cancer Practice,* 2001, *9* (Suppl. 1), S85–91.

National Center for Charitable Statistics. *IRS Form 990 Return Transaction File.* Washington, D.C.: National Center for Charitable Statistics, 1990.

National Center for Charitable Statistics. *IRS Form 990 Return Transaction File.* Washington, D.C.: National Center for Charitable Statistics, 2000.

Patton, M. Q. *Utilization-Focused Evaluation: The New Century Text.* (3rd ed.) Thousand Oaks, Calif.: Sage, 1997.

Preskill, H., and Compton, D. (eds.). "The American Cancer Society's Collaborative Evaluation Fellows Project: A Nationwide Program Evaluation Strategy." *Cancer Practice,* 2001, *9* (Suppl. 1).

Preskill, H., and Torres, R. T. *Evaluative Inquiry for Learning In Organizations.* Thousand Oaks, Calif.: Sage, 1999.

Ritchie, L. A. "The American Cancer Society's Collaborative Evaluation Fellows Project: A Look at the Qualities, Characteristics and Themes of Thirty-Six Evaluation Reports." Unpublished manuscript. Atlanta: American Cancer Society, 2001.

DONALD W. COMPTON *is director of the Division Evaluation Services, American Cancer Society, National Home Office, Atlanta.*

REBECCA GLOVER-KUDON is manager, Division Evaluation Services, American Cancer Society, National Home Office, Atlanta.

IRIS E. SMITH is director, National Evaluation Services, American Cancer Society, National Home Office, Atlanta.

MARY EDEN AVERY is manager, National Evaluation Services, American Cancer Society, National Home Office, Atlanta.

This case study documents two years of ECB in a large midwestern school district and exercizing ECB goals.

4

Building the Evaluation Capacity of a School District

Jean A. King

ECB is a growth industry in local school districts in the United States. The burgeoning use of high- and low-stakes accountability testing mandated by districts and states (and perhaps in the near future by the U.S. Department of Education) has focused attention as never before on individual schools' abilities to increase student achievement, especially their test scores, over time. Administrators and staff can read about their schools' successes or failures in the newspapers, and those that consistently perform poorly may be subject to external intervention, including takeover or "reconstitution." Advances in technology that can bring schools relevant and understandable data that are easy to manipulate, coupled with accountability and accreditation systems that require yearly school improvement plans, point to the importance of infrastructures within schools and district offices to support ongoing evaluation activities.

This case study focuses on the process of building evaluation capacity in a school district from the perspective of an internal evaluator hired explicitly to develop the evaluation function for the district, that is, to carry out ECB. The case example will show how this work was originally conceived and how and why it changed, describing activities over the course of two years and framing the issues facing one school district as it sought to build evaluation capacity. Although other district contexts will vary, the lessons learned in this district may illuminate the challenges confronting any large school system seeking to increase its long-term capacity to conduct and use program evaluations in its everyday activities.

NEW DIRECTIONS FOR EVALUATION, no. 93, Spring 2002   © Wiley Periodicals, Inc.

District Context

With 40 schools and roughly 42,000 students, Anoka-Hennepin Independent School District 11, which comprises thirteen communities northwest of Minnesota's Twin Cities, is the third largest in Minnesota. Unlike the state's two largest districts (Minneapolis and St. Paul), District 11's communities do not face the challenges resulting from being an urban center such as high poverty rates, a high percentage of students who speak English as a second language, and high rates of family disruption. Students do well both on state-mandated tests (grades 3, 5, 8, and 10) and on local school-board-mandated, nationally normed tests (grades 4 and 6), suggesting that the children really *are* above average—an inside joke in Minnesota. Although the district's minority population has doubled in recent years, it is now only 8 percent, and the percentage of students receiving free and reduced-price lunches, while growing, remains comparatively small.

Garrison Keillor of National Public Radio's "Prairie Home Companion" fame graduated from Anoka High School, and Governor Jessie Ventura, whose home is nearby, has helped coach football at another of the district's four high schools. District challenges stem from a low tax base that yields low per-pupil funding, from continuing growth in the district as families move into local communities, and from a sincere commitment to help every student reach the maximum of his or her potential. The current superintendent often states publicly, "We teach all students one child at a time." It is a local school board goal, for example, that all Anoka-Hennepin children will "read independently and well" by the end of third grade, regardless of their skill level when they enter kindergarten.

Although internal program evaluation is a relatively recent addition to district practice, high-quality student assessment is not. The district's Student Assessment Department was created in the mid-1980s when a long-time superintendent hired a charismatic assessment director to expand the testing program into the areas of curriculum and classroom instruction. Under her leadership, the department's activities broadened to include standardized testing, curriculum-managed instruction (CMI), and criterion-referenced testing (CRT) at a number of grades, and the Assurance of Basic Learning (ABL)—a high-stakes test to document basic student learning prior to high school graduation. As the superintendent once stated, "If the movement toward a quantified accountability had not emerged as state public policy, it would have emerged as an Anoka-Hennepin School District effort. Throughout our district's history we have attempted to lead in the field of accountability, not follow." When two educational reforms swept the state (outcome-based education, which morphed into standards-based reform) the district was a leader in developing and piloting performance assessments in a variety of curricular areas. With the addition of state graduation standards and competency tests—including state high school graduation tests in reading, math, and writing—CMI, the CRTs, and ABL were dropped from district practice. The Student Assessment Department remains the administrative unit responsible for increasing numbers of mandated standardized tests, which mushroomed from six different tests in 1996–97 to twelve in 2001–02. Over the years, the work of assessment has become, as one of the staff often quips, "Tests Are Us." While the standardized testing load has doubled, the number of support staff in the department has remained at three.

But as important as student assessment remains, the district superintendent and the associate superintendent for instructional support recognized an equally important role for collecting and compiling information to inform decision making. Two examples point to a central district administration attuned to the value and use of evaluation studies and committed to adding them to district functioning. When two of the district's high schools adopted four-period school days and the other two did not, the district collaborated with the Center for Applied Research and Educational Improvement at the University of Minnesota in an extensive study of this natural experiment (Maruyama and others, 1995). Based on the results, the district ultimately implemented the four-period day at all four of its high schools.

The second example occurred during the 1998–99 school year, when the administration and local teachers union collaborated on a districtwide study of the implementation of graduation standards using the Concerns-Based Adoption Model Survey. The associate superintendent for instructional support presented the survey results at the opening administrative workshop in August 1999 so that building-level administrators could begin the year with current data on their teachers' concerns about implementing state-mandated graduation standards. At that same workshop, the district superintendent announced to everyone, "This district *will* become data-driven," suggesting a notion of evaluation similar to that of Preskill and Torres (1999, p. 1) that "an ongoing process for investigating and understanding critical organizational issues," with the instrumental use of data is integral to the continuing overall process.

At that time, the district had operated without a head of the Student Assessment Department for almost a year. The search for a replacement had ended unsuccessfully, and district leadership sought a creative expansion of the department's function. A teacher on special assignment assumed the role of assessment facilitator, with responsibility for district and state test administration, for biennial district involvement in the National Assessment of Educational Progress (NAEP) and for district-school liaison work on all testing matters. The district then hired as their internal evaluator an individual with more than twenty years' experience in educational evaluation. This new evaluator—a professor on leave from the University of Minnesota—was charged with conducting program evaluations and using them to build the capacity of staff at each of the district's forty schools, as well as in its central Curriculum, Instruction, and Assessment (CIA)

Department, to engage in data-based decision making, or ECB. This task was separate from the testing program (for example, the test orders, training, troubleshooting, and concerned parents). In contrast to evaluators in many districts, the internal evaluator in the Anoka-Hennepin district, given the title of coordinator of research and evaluation, was truly responsible for focusing on the district's capacity to conduct high-quality, useful instructional program evaluations that were indeed to be used at both the district and school level. Central to the coordinator's work was developing a revised "vision" and perhaps a new name for the department, one that incorporated both functions—student assessment and program evaluation and its uses.

This difficult task was made easier by the district's work climate. The professional climate in the central administration is one of mutual respect, trust, and good humor. A central coffee machine and cafeteria foster informal connections and conversations, and several times throughout the year there are buildingwide luncheons and celebrations. Although people take their work extremely seriously, they are encouraged whenever possible to collaborate and to laugh along the way.

Two Challenges of a Large System

One of the challenges facing anyone working in a large bureaucracy is how to get information about and participate meaningfully in relevant activities. In addition to informal connections, the R&E (research and evaluation) coordinator purposefully attended regular meetings of two district administrative groups: the instructional support team (IST), which consists of professional staff who report directly to the associate superintendent for instructional support in addition to appropriate others (for example, the district head of HR); and the instructional facilitators (IF), twenty or so teachers on special assignment who provide subject-specific curricular support, as well as ongoing facilitation to one of four clusters of District 11 schools (one grade 9–12 high school and its elementary and middle feeder schools). In addition, she sat on four standing district committees that met monthly:

- Graduation standards implementation committee (GSIC)—the committee the school board charged with monitoring the implementation of the Minnesota Graduation Standards
- Blueprint (for literacy) implementation committee (BIC)—a committee overseeing the district's move (K–5) to a balanced literacy instructional approach
- Curriculum advisory committee (CAC)—the committee monitoring the district's overall curriculum development and implementation process, which is important in a district with a highly centralized K–12 curriculum
- Systems accountability committee (SAC)—a state-mandated citizens' review group that prepares an annual report for the district school board and the public on the status of education in the district, including student achievement results and the results of curriculum reviews

Participation in these meetings proved invaluable because it enabled the internal evaluator to monitor what was happening in this large system and to connect with various aspects of curriculum, instruction, and assessment across the district without attempting to be a visible presence at the forty schools. Shortly after her arrival, the coordinator received good advice: Do not plan to visit each building because even one or two trips to a school during the year (a total of forty to eighty site visits) would not satisfy staff there that an outsider (especially an evaluator who is at once a frightening and powerful stranger) knew their school more than superficially—and they would be right.

By participating in these meetings, the coordinator met key district stakeholders and worked to understand potential evaluation issues affecting instructional change. During year one, these meetings helped her develop an awareness of the complexity of the district and of the status and effectiveness of the evaluation function therein—where it might be added, fostered, or otherwise changed. For example, conversations with the district's head of diversity led eventually to the planning of a developmental evaluation of the district's diversity committee's goals, which an advanced doctoral student at the University of Minnesota is conducting. This project will eventually collect annual survey data on cultural literacy to monitor its development in both students and staff. (The work is also closely aligned with the external evaluation of the district's Desegregation Plan.) Meeting participation also created opportunities and communication of ideas about ECB in the district, including evaluation studies and their use in decision making at the school and district level. For example, before the release of results of the massive Graduation Standards Implementation Study (described next), the graduation standards implementation committee spent a lengthy meeting reviewing the data and checking claims based on them—a useful activity because it brought them face-to-face with the realities of the study's outcomes, that is, the realities to which they had to respond. This was use in practice and practice in use.

A second and more district-specific challenge came from staffing issues that affected all evaluation and ECB activities. First, although the Assessment Department workload had increased dramatically over the years, its staffing had not, resulting in frustration and anger for an extremely talented support staff. The staffing included five positions: two professional positions (the student assessment facilitator and the new coordinator of research and evaluation) and three "Class B" secretaries. These secretaries, whose positions were part of the secretarial union, were extremely competent people whose jobs required a high level of technical skill (for example, maintaining and manipulating large databases, using a number of complex software packages, preparing tables of quantitative data, interacting with schools, the public, and the state department) but whose duties prevented the reclassification of their positions to a higher level and a salary commensurate with the level of work (for example, they did not supervise anyone other than temporary clerical help).

Between 1998 and 2001, the Assessment Office earned the unfortunate reputation as a training site for other offices and agencies. Five secretaries cycled through the office: two moved to another district where they received better positions and sizable salary increases; one, frustrated after more than a year of trying to have her position upgraded, made a lateral move to a school; two took jobs in private industry. These changes left the office short one secretary for most of the 2000–01 school year, even as the workload increased due to the coordinator's evaluation and ECB activities. The constant deadlines and inevitable falling behind created a highly stressful work environment for the year.

A related staffing challenge concerned the supervision of department staff. Given the nature of their contracts, neither the assessment facilitator nor the R&E coordinator was allowed to directly supervise the support staff, which meant that the three secretaries reported to the director of curriculum, instruction, and assessment (CIA), even though the facilitator and coordinator were directing their work. Because of the personalities involved and the collaborative culture of the district office, the staff worked around these potentially confusing lines of formal authority. But the greatest success of the Fall 2000 semester—thanks to the efforts of the associate superintendent—was the reclassification of one clerical staff position to a nonbargaining-unit, office coordinator position. The person in that position now supervises the two remaining secretaries. In the proposed staffing for a reconstituted Evaluation, Assessment, and Research (EAR) Office, a full-time director of evaluation, assessment, and research would supervise both the assessment facilitator and the office coordinator. However, two factors have put that on hold for the foreseeable future: the board's traditional reluctance to add central office administrators and the grim budget situation for precollegiate education in Minnesota. A district that pink-slipped 130 teachers in May 2001 is unlikely to hire an assessment and evaluation supervisor in the months following.

Two Years of ECB Work (1999–2001)

Over the course of two school years (1999–2000 and 2000–2001), the coordinator collaborated with people both within and outside the school district to bring ECB goals to life in the district, and what follows is a progress report as the ECB effort enters its third year. During Fall 1999, the new R&E coordinator, with the support of the associate superintendent, developed a vision for the Assessment Department—an ECB plan that focused on four goals. The first was to develop staff commitment and skills in program evaluation and its use through participation in model evaluations of key district initiatives each year. This goal served two functions, one related to ECB and the other to program evaluation: (1) to engage people and teach them the logic and procedures of evaluation studies through an interactive process of evaluation (see Patton, 1997) and (2) to provide solid data for decision making in important and visible areas of curriculum, instruction, and assessment.

The second ECB goal was to build an infrastructure for data collection, analysis, and presentation that would support program evaluation within the system. This infrastructure had to include the following capacities: (1) to generate and process surveys with quantitative and qualitative items, (2) to conduct focus groups and analyze their data, (3) to collect and compile student work, and (4) to prepare both oral and written evaluation reports. Partly related to the second, the third goal was to facilitate the existing school improvement process (SIP) by developing a system of school-level reporting to provide principals and teachers data about their schools, including existing test data and the results of SIP activities. Ideally, school staff would ultimately be able to customize SIP data collection, based on specific goals for their students. The final ECB goal—to create a network of teachers, administrators, and other staff across the district who would routinize classroom- or school-based inquiry—represented the coordinator's greatest hope: that the processes of program evaluation and its use would become integral to the way individual district personnel went about their work, making evaluation part and parcel of their ongoing activities.

Goal 1. The first goal was *to develop staff commitment and skills in program evaluation and its use.* The expanded Assessment Department's first function—to develop staff commitment and skills through participation in model evaluations of key district initiatives—in essence killed two birds with one stone. Instructional decision makers in the central office wanted solid data each year on the implementation and outcomes of specific initiatives designed to increase student achievement. At the same time, by using a participatory process to design and conduct these evaluations, district staff who took part would learn over time how to frame evaluation questions, how to put together data-collection instruments, how to make claims using data, how to use data in their everyday work, and so on. Two examples— one an evaluation of the implementation of Minnesota's graduation rule and the other a self-study of special education in the district—document how these model evaluations supported the ECB process.

During the 1999–2000 school year, the Graduation Standards Study produced extensive evaluation data using multiple methods, including two surveys (all administrators and Graduation Standards representatives in each building) and two rounds of focus groups (teachers nominated as exemplars of standards-based instruction and high school students experiencing standards-based education). Four components of the study purposefully engaged people in ways that would teach them about the evaluation process. First, the fifteen members of the graduation standards implementation committee, which was responsible for the implementation, reviewed the previous year's survey data and the concerns of the various groups they represented to collaboratively frame the study's questions. Throughout the year, they monitored the study's progress at their monthly meetings, suggesting changes as needed. The second ECB component developed when it became clear that focus groups would help to answer one of the committee's questions and that the Assessment Department staff was unable to conduct enough groups to ensure widespread participation across the district. A group of instructional facilitators volunteered for training on how to conduct focus groups and then assisted in eighteen teacher groups and independently led sixteen student groups in the process, creating a cadre of experienced focus group facilitators for the district. Third, the committee sponsored a discussion session to which every teacher who participated in a focus group was invited. Hosted by the superintendent, the meeting content included oral and written presentations of the focus group results, followed by small-group discussion by the teachers to clarify and amplify the meaning of the data. In these discussions, teachers not only learned about others' perceptions of the Graduation Standards implementation but about the analysis of focus group data and the ways data could support district-level decisions. Fourth, as noted earlier, near the end of the year GSIC members engaged in an interactive analysis and discussion of the data, suggesting implications for the continued Graduation Standards implementation. They decided that the data collected were so extensive that no additional data would be required during the next academic year.

A self-study of the Special Education Department also supported ECB by developing two processes that are now integral to the district's evaluation function: a viable way to organize large-scale participatory studies and an interactive, cost-effective means of collecting qualitative data. Owing to the highly political nature of special education in the district, the self-study team had an initial membership of over one hundred people (representatives from different grade levels, roles, disabilities, and so on), fifty of whom eventually attended monthly meetings for over a year. The district coordinator worked with two external consultant-facilitators to design a participatory process for all phases of the evaluation study. In so doing, they developed a two-part structure that has become the model for all large studies in the district: (1) a six- to eight-person data collection team (DCT), made up of district personnel most closely involved with the study's focus, and (2) a much larger study committee (thirty to fifty people) that frames questions, analyzes data, and makes recommendations. The DCT was responsible for the nuts and bolts of carrying out the study—inviting people to meetings, following up on absences, compiling existing data, arranging logistics, and so forth. Relying on methods borrowed from cooperative learning, the monthly meetings of the study committee were devoted to short presentations, table teamwork on data analysis, and the development of claims based on the data, and eventual creation and prioritizing of recommendations. Those who participated in the study committee reported that they enjoyed both the special education content of the process and what they had learned about evaluation through their participation.

A second capacity-building process emerged of necessity during the course of the study. Given budget constraints, parental focus groups were simply not feasible. But whether they were costly or not, the study committee believed they were needed in order to allow parents' voices to be heard. In response, the evaluation consultants devised a cost-effective adaptation of focus group methodology, first labeled "dialogue groups" (since renamed "data dialogues"), in which small groups of two or three participants discussed questions related to the study, then recorded their own data. In this way, large numbers of people were able to give data and simultaneously have a good conversation with other parents. Other evaluations in the district (for example, the teacher induction program evaluation, a study of middle school implementation) have since used the data-dialogue process both to foster meaningful discussion of issues and to generate qualitative data in a manner the district can afford.

After two years of studies, then, the first ECB goal of developing evaluation capacity in the district through participation in the evaluations of key initiatives had resulted in increased capacity in several ways. The members of certain committees accepted responsibility for working on evaluations of their activities, and over three hundred district staff, students, and parents had helped to manage or participate actively in one or more evaluations, learning about the process en route. In addition, a viable structure emerged for conducting effective evaluation studies with limited resources. During the 2001–02 school year, potential topics of inquiry (for example, the implementation of balanced literacy, the secondary advanced learner, and the "disengaged" learner) created additional opportunities for such capacity building.

Goal 2. The second goal was *to build an infrastructure for data collection, analysis, and presentation that would support program evaluation and its use within the district.* As noted earlier, this infrastructure needed to include the capacity to create and analyze high-quality data on any number of topics and to craft effective reports for intended users. Two components added to the infrastructure have been discussed—the instructional facilitators trained to conduct and analyze focus groups and the "data dialogue process"—both of which increased the district's capacity to collect qualitative data. The true challenge stemmed from the survey work that had been the department's responsibility for a number of years in support of the state-mandated curriculum review and other surveys. Historically, instructional facilitators had compiled teacher and student survey items, which Assessment Department clerical staff then copied onto computer forms. Once respondents returned the forms to the office, they were scanned and data summaries given to the appropriate facilitators. Although it was not a primary responsibility, department staff also facilitated the administration of other surveys on occasion.

In the context of ECB in a large district, the need for an effective way to routinely conduct surveys was heightened, but during these two years, computer hardware and software failure led to great frustration on the part of many people—Assessment Department staff primary among them. For over a decade, the Assessment Department had used the same software to scan and analyze bubbled data sheets, successfully keeping the survey system alive even when newer programs became available. In fact, by the year 2000 the company that originally wrote the scanning software no longer provided technical support for it, so there was no external help when something went wrong. During the course of the first summer, it became clear that this system was on its last legs—staff who had previously been able to coax the machine to cooperate were no longer able to do so, and scanning became a highly uninviting and time-consuming experience for those responsible. At times, the equipment simply wouldn't work and projects sat unfinished. Unfortunately, the cost of a new system was far beyond the department budget, so for about a month during the summer it seemed there was no solution. The hero of this story was the district's head of technology, who had a continuous improvement mind-set and fully understood the importance of having an efficient survey process in the Assessment Department. With support from the associate superintendent, authorization was given for the purchase of state-of-the art scanning equipment and software; it was installed within the month.

Unfortunately, as is often the case, this good news was accompanied by some bad news: the expensive new equipment and software had equally expensive (and non-negotiable) training—over $2,000 per person, plus expenses. Such an expenditure for even one person was unimaginable in the department's existing budget. And even if the department had had the money, staff turnover made such an investment seem risky. So during the 2000–01 school year, the exciting new possibilities became limited to what staff were able to figure out by reading the manual and calling the company's less-than-responsive help line. They quickly figured out how to do straightforward scanning, but any subtleties or complexities created impossible challenges. In July 2001, CIA leadership paid for one secretary to attend four days of training, and, not surprisingly, the department's survey productivity increased dramatically. Cross-training of other Assessment Department staff in the near future will provide appropriate technical back-up.

Goal 3. The third goal was *to facilitate the existing school improvement process (SIP)*. This would be done by developing and implementing a system of school-based reporting to provide principals and teachers data about their schools and the results of SIP activities. Over time, the data would be customized; the principals and teachers would help create it. In Anoka-Hennepin, the central administration required building-level school improvement teams to submit school improvement plans by October 15 each year, which the appropriate area superintendents then reviewed. The plans included goals, indicators, strategies, a time line, and so on, and site teams were encouraged to review and reflect on outcomes at the end of the year. In practice, however, the plans differed widely, with little formal accountability. Some schools took on multiple goals and listed fifteen to twenty strategies for reaching them; others wrote lists of ongoing activities (for example, staff attending workshops, meetings being held to discuss certain topics) with little visible pay-off in terms of outcomes. Most buildings listed increased reading or math test scores as indicators of progress, but the link between the strategy and the outcome was rarely explicit, that is, no explicit logic model was in place. In short, the district school improvement process was in essence a hollow evaluation process—goals were set, strategies implemented, and data collected but with little support or accountability for the results. An ECB assumption was that providing all available data to a school on an annual basis might prove useful for both building and central administrators.

As the assessment staff set about developing reports, however, they came to understand why these had never been done in the district. They quickly learned that student databases were purged over the summer, and data not stored prior to the purge might be lost. Other data were inaccessible without time-consuming work (for example, they were in teachers' grade books locked in school vaults). Even data the staff knew existed weren't necessarily readily accessible because one of the hard drives in the Assessment Department had crashed a year earlier and lost all of its memory, some of which was not backed up. Other data needed for the reports (for example, on attendance and dropouts) were available only in other departments in the central district office. Because staff in those offices were already fully occupied with their own jobs, they had little incentive to generate data for the Assessment Department, often putting the request in an "eventual" pile with other such requests ("We'll add it to our list of things to do"). A final and obvious challenge related to the packaging and use of data for school improvement was extremely practical: many of the staff in the district had old Apple computers and software, making it difficult to send them information electronically in any form that they could easily access or use. These problems, coupled with the department context of understaffing and overwork, meant that the building reports unavoidably received low priority.

Despite the many challenges, however, department staff (assisted by temporary clerical help) did succeed in creating data reports for all elementary schools in Fall 2000 and again in Summer 2001. During the 2000–01 school year, a technology facilitator began work on an electronic form for the district's school improvement plans. As the 2001–02 school year began, two forces were likely to drive the development of a workable school improvement planning process: (1) the state had instituted a process of mandatory school improvement for schools receiving Title I funds and not meeting the criteria of "Annual Yearly Progress," and (2) the associate superintendents instituted changes that would provide support to schools and then hold them more accountable for the results of their annual school improvement activities.

Goal 4. The fourth and final goal was *to create a network of people across the district to routinize classroom- or school-based inquiry*. This goal remained part of a vision but was not yet implemented. Some of the components to support the implementation were in place: (1) many committed professionals who were used to collaboration and were eager to make sense of their practice, (2) issues ripe for practitioner study (for example, the integration of Graduation Standards into the curriculum, (3) the shift to a balanced literacy program in grades K–2, (4) the status of gifted and talented students in the district, (5) technical support available in the Assessment Department, and (6) leadership eager to support such activities.

But major deterrents continued to block progress. First, there were too few days of substitute teacher support available and little money available to release teachers for this purpose. Second, and more important, there were other priorities for staff development more directly related to instructional changes the district sought. Although practitioner research could support the implementation of virtually any change (it is a cost-effective form of professional development), in the district context it lacked the significance of the major studies, the importance of the survey function, or the centrality of the school improvement process.

After two years then, the Assessment Department's ECB goals remained in place, and some progress was evident:

- Several studies had made the department's evaluation activities visible across the district.
- A viable model for structuring the major annual studies was in place.
- Over three hundred people had actively taken part in at least one evaluation study, and literally thousands had completed surveys.
- Central office administrators were refocusing attention on the school improvement process.
- The Assessment Department (once again fully staffed) was able to prepare student data for building use.
- New technology had upgraded the department's survey function.

In the words of the assessment facilitator who sometimes concluded presentations about the department: "Yesterday we stood at the edge of a great abyss. Today we take a giant step forward."

Lessons Learned

This case has focused on two years of a district's efforts to build evaluation capacity. To frame a discussion of what has been learned through the process, however, it is critical to emphasize the Assessment Department's core function: managing the district's standardized testing program. A dozen times during the academic year, the department office was filled almost to the ceiling with boxes containing that month's test; walking in the office became difficult, owing to the number of cardboard cartons arranged in ways to make a fire marshal cringe. These tests ranged from a standardized test of music aptitude given each year to every 4th grader in the district (approximately three thousand students), to formal district writing assessments at two grade levels (approximately six thousand students), to state tests of reading, mathematics, and writing (which over thirteen thousand students take). Department staff attended to details of test distribution and administration because errors, although sometimes unavoidable, were never acceptable. Dire consequences attended certain mistakes, so when the time for each testing approached, the staff's focus did not waiver. Testing came first. In this context, program evaluation and ECB were additions to a departmental plate already chock-full.

Early in the coordinator's tenure in the district, she assumed that the Assessment Department would sponsor formal workshops on evaluation or at least on standardized testing and how to use test data for instructional and school improvement. In the context of Graduation Standards and the implementation of other instructional strategies, however, such workshops made little sense; only the coordinator saw evaluation training as an important priority. Her initial scan found formal program evaluation activities in four places in the district office: (1) staff routinely completed evaluation requirements for federal programs and other grants; (2) instructional facilitators conducted curriculum studies, as mandated by the state, that included surveys and other data collection; (3) the Vocational Education Department commissioned a follow-up study of the graduates of one of the four district high schools each year in order to have data for future grants, and (4) on a regular basis one of the central office administrators commissioned an outside consultant or agency to conduct a study for a specific purpose (for example, the Graduation Standards implementation, areas that voters might support in a tax levy to raise district funding levels, and parents' desires for desegregation planning). In a striking parallel to evaluation in developing countries, it was often outside forces—funding agencies or the state—that either mandated or inspired formal evaluation activity in the district.

In a system where priority items competed for limited resources, this approach to evaluation was sensible. District staff conducted mandatory evaluations or evaluations thought likely to result in practical outcomes. Given competing demands, the notion of evaluation for continuous improvement or as a way of life—although extremely appealing on the conceptual level—was necessarily a harder sell in practice. It is true that the district superintendent wanted to move in this direction and that the annual SIP modeled such a process, but the informal nature of SIP accountability to date meant that building site teams were typically responsible for activities rather than outcomes, creating the possibility of their going through yearly evaluation motions. In retrospect, the prospects for ECB were clear. In the language of the Joint Committee's standards, feasibility was paramount: if program evaluation processes were not made viable in this setting, they simply would not catch on.

Because program evaluation could not be the primary Assessment Department role, the tasks facing the R&E coordinator were threefold. The first related directly to program evaluation: it was the coordinator's job—and only hers—to conduct program evaluations, thereby providing evaluation data for use centrally by district leadership. A key question over time was what might motivate other district staff to voluntarily engage in evaluation activities while acknowledging that, absent a major input of resources, this would necessarily be a long-term effort. The coordinator's other tasks, therefore, related to ECB: (1) creating an infrastructure to support evaluation (ECB Goal 2, including facilitating data collection, helping staff to compile existing data, providing support for framing studies, and so on), and (2) simultaneously creating ongoing evaluation learning opportunities for district staff at all levels (ECB Goals 1, 3, and 4). For almost twenty years, the coordinator had framed her evaluation practice as an instructional activity, applying the four commonplaces of learning—teacher, students, curriculum, and context—to program evaluation (King, 1982). This framework provides a useful structure for discussing the ECB lessons learned in two years.

Teachers. In an ECB effort, the evaluator must become a teacher who purposefully structures evaluation and related activities and continuing collective reflection on these over time. Building capacity requires that the evaluator is integrally connected to people's work and alert to the programs that are potential objects for inquiry because they are key to district functioning, that is, to increasing student achievement. Interpersonal skills and the ability to identify and frame organizational issues are essential. Because relatively few districts have evaluators on staff, professional development is important, and quality program evaluation, especially when it uses participatory processes, can provide such training in situ while at the same time generating useful data.

There are other "teachers" in the ECB process: organizational leaders (administrators and opinion leaders) who make a visible commitment to evaluation, also known as the clout factor (King and Pechman, 1984). They can do this by providing verbal support in public situations (for example, when the superintendent hosted an evaluation meeting) and, more important, by serving as role models who study their own programs and practice. As examples, the superintendent commissioned the development of a districtwide parent satisfaction survey, and the associate superintendent for instructional support consistently "talked the talk and walked the walk" in her many initiatives. In the Anoka-Hennepin school district, staff knew that central office administrators expected to increase data-based decision making and that program evaluation was integral to that process.

Students. In this case, the "students" in ECB were district staff, and the long-term goal was that everyone become an evaluator to some extent, working to make sense of his or her own practice. For this to happen, the evaluator-teacher must provide support and guidance so that evaluation is not just one more thing added to an already packed workload. Motivation and incentives are important, as staff will invariably ask (whether or not they say so out loud) what evaluation can offer them. Distrust of the evaluation process was surprisingly common, even in a district with good intentions; building-level staff nevertheless asked how the data would affect them, who would see the data, and whether these evaluation activities would be "one more thing that is dropped after a year or two." Trust can only be established over time, and in a large organization it remains a fragile commodity.

In addition, people must be able to get information they want and can use, not just what is readily available (for example, standardized test scores that may not relate to their questions of interest). They must also have the power to use evaluation results to make appropriate changes. This can be challenging in a large bureaucracy where someone may blithely propose a change in someone else's arena (for example, middle school students whose data clearly supported longer times for moving between classes and for lunch) or where certain situations are unchangeable, given existing resources (for example, expanding media center staffing in the elementary schools). To the extent that evaluation processes can be integrated seamlessly into ongoing activities (for example, setting up routine survey data collection and analysis), staff may even welcome them. The obvious danger in a system short on evaluation resources, however, is to create more demand than the Assessment Department could realistically handle. There is a delicate balance between creating demand and meeting expectations in a substantive and timely manner.

Curriculum. The curriculum in an ECB effort is the process of continuing evaluation itself, that is, teaching people the cycle and requisite skills of question framing, data collection and analysis, reflection, and planning for the next cycle. Formal training is not necessary because, for many, the evaluation process is fairly intuitive, and in school districts there are typically people familiar with it who are willing to take part. Training may well speed ECB, and targeted training of certain evaluation skills (for example, facilitation using cooperative learning techniques, focus group facilitation, involvement of minority stakeholders) could prove helpful.

The curricular goal is to institutionalize a shared commitment to program evaluation and a culture that includes the purposeful socialization of newcomers to the district. Two things became clear in the case study: (1) that every evaluation project, especially those involving people across buildings, became an instructional opportunity and (2) that participatory methods using small teams and work groups could provide nonthreatening, hands-on learning experiences. Having an established structure for these participatory studies is one indicator of district ECB. The Middle School Study used the management and participation structure that evolved during the Special Education Study, with the guidance of skilled outside facilitators but on a smaller and more cost-effective scale (thirty people rather than fifty and using a salaried, in-house facilitator). This beta test with the same structure but using a shorter time line and no external resources demonstrated the capacity to conduct a participatory evaluation of a major initiative, although the department's being short-staffed and using new software that no one understood created overwhelming practical challenges.

Assessment must be part of the ECB curriculum, that is, establishing and tracking indicators, which in a district environment might include the following:

- *Inputs*—fiscal support (increased staffing and resources devoted to evaluation that are built into the budget and are not the first thing to be cut, even in dire times)
- *Processes*—the in-house capacity to collect and analyze data, create usable reports, and involve people in discussion; a framework for potential studies (a structure in place to generate new studies, support the process, and use data); an accessible process and support for anyone who wants to conduct a study; the ability to capture and compile the data for use (staff and data processing capacity); and purposeful socialization into the evaluation process
- Outcomes—increased demand for existing data; widespread involvement by numerous people in different types of studies; references to data during meetings; and ongoing use of data throughout the organization.

Context. In the context of a school district in the United States, at least for the foreseeable future, program evaluation will remain secondary to administering standardized tests and reporting their results. As noted, standardized testing was the core activity for the Assessment Department, demanding resources and a staff schedule with deadlines that allow little flexibility. The one secretary who worked on survey data was pulled off evaluation work if she was needed for a testing task. In other words, the standardized testing program easily—and typically—overwhelms the program evaluation function (King, forthcoming). To build evaluation capacity in a district setting, ECB practitioners cannot ignore this context, especially as the stakes for testing increase in a context of highly visible public accountability.

School districts, however, do need access to evaluation expertise, both internal and external. Structural conditions can support the development of evaluation capacity: (1) time to collaborate including, when possible, being physically together in an environment separate from the interruptions of the school day; (2) meaningful incentives for participation; (3) opportunities for reflection; and (4) effective communication (for example, the district practice of key messages summarized from important meetings and standardized "action minutes" that document meeting content, decisions, and who will do what next). In a district context, the Joint Committee Standards' categories of utility and feasibility highlight the fact that ECB must be both useful and workable, targeting programs that are central to improved student achievement and making visible use of data over time.[1] "Low hanging fruit"—visible, easily made changes—provides evidence that the evaluation process can lead to improvement (for example, reduced Graduation Standards requirements after teacher survey data recommended that, or heightened parent communication in Special Education when data documented such a need).

Final Reflection: To ECB or Not to ECB?

Some people may read this case study and offer condolences for two years of work with a seemingly unhappy ending. People did not deflect efforts at building evaluation capacity; they don't need to because the context itself makes it exceedingly difficult (for example, next year's budget situation). What's missing (for sure) is time, the ability to get people together, incentives for participation, and even better communication, which the size of the district impedes.

But such a reading would be incorrect. Has the district built and sustained sufficient and appropriate evaluation capacity for its needs and wants? This case provides an example of the definition by Stockdill, Baizerman, and Compton (Chapter One, this volume) of ECB as "intentional work to constantly co-create and co-sustain an overall process that makes quality evaluation and its uses routine in organizations and systems." Even in light of a dire budget situation—including the potential for a second year of budget cuts, perhaps of as much as $10 million—the ECB effort in Anoka-Hennepin has not ended; top administrators and staff are committed to its continued development. A district staff person once commented, "In a big system, you can only do big things." To commit to ECB is a big thing, and Anoka-Hennepin Independent School District 11 is happily two years closer to this goal.

Note

1. In a district setting, the JCS category of propriety is a given, the sine qua non of any program evaluation effort.

References

King, J. A. "Studying the Local Use of Evaluation: A Discussion of Theoretical Issues and an Empirical Study." *Studies in Educational Evaluation,* 1982, *8,* 175–183.

King, J. A. *Proposal for an Expanded Assessment Department.* Coon Rapids, Minn.: Anoka-Hennepin Independent School District 11, 2001.

King, J. A. "Evaluating Educational Programs and Projects in the USA. In D. S. (ed.), *International Handbook of Educational Evaluation,* forthcoming.

King, J. A., and Pechman, E. M. "Pinning a Wave to the Shore: Conceptualizing School Evaluation Use." *Educational Evaluation and Policy Analysis,* 1984, *6*(3), 241–251.

Maruyama, G., Freeman, C., Hole, D., Frederickson, J., and Springis-Doss, R. *Study of the Four Period Schedule for Anoka-Hennepin No. 11.* Minneapolis, Minn.: Center for

Applied Research and Educational Improvement, College of Education and Human Development, University of Minnesota, 1995.

Patton, M. Q. *Utilization-Focused Evaluation.* (3rd ed.) Thousand Oaks, Calif.: Sage, 1997.

Preskill, H., and Torres, R. T. *Evaluative Inquiry for Learning in Organizations.* Thousand Oaks, Calif.: Sage, 1999.

JEAN A. KING is an associate professor in the Department of Educational Policy and Administration, College of Education and Human Development, University of Minnesota, Minneapolis.

5

The World Bank promotes ECB within developing countries, many of which have modest human resource capacities. The World Bank's ECB efforts are fairly recent, but a range of experience and case studies is rapidly being developed. The contrasts among these cases provides many valuable lessons about the requirements for successful ECB, defined here as the creation of a sustained system that ensures the conduct of evaluation and its intensive use.

The World Bank's ECB Experience

Keith Mackay[1]

The World Bank's Operations Evaluation Department employs about sixty evaluation staff and has had an ECB program since 1987. For the first decade of its existence, the ECB program involved the part-time efforts of a single staffer, with the strong support of the vice president responsible for the Operations Evaluation Department (OED), working with individual governments interested in ECB. It was only in 1999 that a staffer was given the full-time task of ECB. By early 2001, ECB work was being undertaken in other parts of the World Bank and in about ten countries, and that number of countries is growing rapidly.

The primary focus in this case study is on the ECB outreach activities of the World Bank (hereafter, "the Bank"), involving provision of advice and assistance to individual governments. But it is also necessary to understand the many challenges in achieving acceptance of the priority for ECB within the Bank. So there are two stories to be told here. The main one involves the many ECB lessons being learned through working with a range of governments in diverse and difficult environments. The subsidiary story is how ECB is becoming a recognized and valued activity within the Bank itself.

The Role of the Bank

Both stories can be elucidated by understanding the nature and role of the Bank. It is owned by about 180 developed and developing countries and makes about $15 billion of new loans each year; poverty reduction is an overall objective. With a staff of almost 11,000, it manages a total lending portfolio of some $206 billion. The Bank works in more than 100 developing countries, in all sectors and many thematic areas, including health, education, environment, agriculture, infrastructure, private sector, and governance.

The Bank is sometimes perceived as a monolithic organization filled with buttoned-down, hard-nosed bankers interested only in the bottom line. The truth is very different. The Bank has something of the flavor of a large university faculty with a wide range of interests and areas of expertise: economists, sector and thematic experts in areas such as health, education, transport, the environment, agriculture, energy, urban development, governance and, yes, the odd evaluator. The Bank's staff are fully committed to its poverty-reduction mission but are fully extended and feel they have to cope with a growing multitude of corporate priorities. The Bank operates internally as a marketplace of competing ideas; there are spirited debates about the latest thinking on development issues (Picciotto, 2001). Those of us working in specialist areas who are advocating new ideas and areas for attention (such as ECB) have to rise above the clamor of the crowd and seek to gain attention and acceptance for our work.

The Bank's influence on its client-country governments rests substantially on its ability to make loans at concessional rates of interest; for the poorest countries, Bank loans are interest-free. This provides the Bank considerable leverage in influencing the policies of governments. But over and above this influence is the Bank's intellectual role as a source of expertise and advice on development issues; the Bank's regular surveys of its clients suggest that most governments value this role highly.

A major area of emphasis for the Bank is governance, broadly defined as the nature, roles, capacities, and performance of government. Throughout the 1990s, there was a growing and significant emphasis on this broad area, and it became much more widely appreciated within the international development community that the quality of a country's governance arrangements is a powerful determinant of the success of its poverty-reduction efforts (World Bank, 1997a). Key governance issues that have been emphasized in recent years include

- Efforts to fight corruption in developing countries
- Civil service reform, including a merit-based civil service (sometimes with performance contracts for senior civil servants)
- Fundamental, zero-based reviews of public sector functions
- Better national budget systems, including performance budgeting
- Capacity building across the entire range of civil service functions
- Participation by civil society in determining national priorities and to help ensure the accountability of government

A common theme of many of these areas of governance is a focus on the *performance* of government.

These governance priorities provide the context for the Bank's ECB work; they also require that a broad range of M&E tools be available for use within countries. The choice of which tools are most appropriate for any individual country will depend on a range of factors such as existing capacities (strengths and weaknesses), on national priorities as to what types of M&E information would be most useful or most immediately available, and perhaps most important of all, on the relative cost-effectiveness of the various M&E tools, methods, and approaches that could be used. These include program evaluation and review, cost-benefit analysis, performance indicators and logframe analysis, theory-based evaluation, rapid review, process evaluations, service delivery surveys, public expenditure tracking surveys, participatory evaluation, and meta-analysis of existing M&E findings.

Thus ECB in the Bank, which uses a slightly different shorthand title, *evaluation capacity development (ECD),* encompasses a broad range of evaluative tools and approaches that include but go beyond program evaluation.

The purpose of the Bank's ECB efforts is not to build M&E capacities per se; capacity building is simply one step along a "results chain" (which is discussed later). The Bank's view is unequivocally that use of M&E results is necessary for "ECB success": if a country is able to increase the availability of monitoring information and evaluation findings but this evidence is not used, the ECB efforts will have failed.

To those who work in the area of evaluation, the information and understanding that M&E can provide should have natural and obvious uses:

- As an aid to sound management within government ministries and agencies—the learning function of M&E
- To enlighten and support government policymaking and planning by providing information on the likely benefits and costs of alternative policies, programs, and projects
- To provide evidence in relation to the accountability of governments to civil society and to others

The value of these potential uses of M&E might be self-evident to evaluators, but this value is much less apparent to others in the Bank or in client countries. Hence one focus of the Bank's ECB work has been to explain the various uses of M&E and the ways in which the performance focus of M&E can support many different areas of governance reform.

The ECB Process: Achieving Acceptance Within the World Bank

The history of the Bank's ECB efforts has had three main stages. The first ran from 1987 to 1997 and stemmed from the objective of strengthening public sector management within countries that borrow from the Bank. During this period, OED provided ECB support to individual governments in response to their specific requests (World Bank, 1994). It also disseminated lessons from its ECB experience (Operations Evaluation Department,

1994). OED's support reflected its strong commitment to M&E and the Bank's long history of support for other types of capacity building in developing countries. The Bank's board has noted that ECB is part of OED's formal mandate. The Bank's approach to evaluation is outlined in the next section.

The second stage in the Bank's ECB work ran from 1997 to 1999. This work drew on the experience of developed countries such as Australia and Canada, which had mandated evaluation as a core government activity (Mackay, 1998a). During this period, OED devoted more time and effort to persuading key, senior Bank staff about the merits of ECB and persuading the evaluation offices of other multilateral and bilateral donors such as the African Development Bank (ADB), the Swiss Agency for Development and Cooperation (SDC), the Norwegian Foreign Affairs Ministry, and the UNDP to actively support ECB efforts (for example, Picciotto, 1999). These persuasion efforts were led by the vice president who oversees OED and who is strongly committed to ECB.

Evaluation Activities at the World Bank

The Bank has a long history of involvement in evaluation. It has produced evaluation methodologies and handbooks of world-class quality, especially concerning project evaluation (economic cost-benefit analysis; for example, Squire and Van der Tak, 1975; Gittinger, 1982). Since 1972, the Bank has also had formal requirements that have ensured the preparation of self-evaluation reports for all Bank-financed projects and other operations as soon as they have been completed; these reports are largely prepared by the Bank's own country teams and other operational areas, although in formal terms they are prepared jointly with the borrower government. In the past, the quality of these self-evaluation reports was variable, and therefore considerable efforts have been made in recent years to strengthen them and to strengthen ex ante evaluation and review. Most of these self-evaluations have involved rapid review, but more rigorous program evaluations have also been conducted (for some examples, see Baker, 2000). The Bank also has a system of quality-assurance panels.

OED, which is an independent unit and has existed since 1975, reports directly to the Bank's board of directors and evaluates a rolling sample of Bank operations (Operations Evaluation Department, 1998); the board is highly appreciative of OED's evaluations. OED has made its evaluation reports more learning-oriented to ensure their utilization in the Bank's operational work. And OED has linked its evaluation agenda more closely to the priorities of country teams, in terms of thematic and country focus, and has ensured that evaluation results are available in a timely manner to feed into the preparation of new projects and other Bank operations; it has prepared shorter, more readable evaluation reports, and it prepares multiple media for dissemination of evaluation findings, including evaluation reports, précis, and seminars and through Web sites such as worldbank.org/html/oed/.

The high profile and credibility of OED among the development evaluation community facilitated the development of ECB partnerships with
other donor organizations. An example of how this collaboration has been
pursued is the international seminars provided for senior government officials and donors, such as one held in Washington, D.C., in 1998 (Mackay
1998b) and another held the same year in Abidjan, Côte d'Ivoire (African
Development Bank and OED, 1999). These seminars raised awareness about
the potential role of M&E in sound governance, and they strengthened
interest in ECB. Such efforts paid off in terms of ECB being initiated with
substantive OED support in Ghana and Uganda; the nature of this country-
based work is described later in this chapter.

In parallel with these high-level awareness-raising efforts, OED staff
were also active in a number of related Bank activities, seeking to raise the
profile and merits of M&E: speaking on ECB at seminars and training
courses on issues such as the role of M&E in national budget systems, and
participating in the Bank's thematic groups where experts on particular topics (for example, civil service reform, budget systems, NGOs, and civil society participation) meet and discuss latest issues.

A related strand of OED activity was more educational in nature—the
preparation and dissemination of ECB resource material with the objective
of learning from past experience and of trying to make ECB less of an art
and more of a science. This resource material includes publication of seminar proceedings, a diagnostic guide and action framework for ECB
(Mackay, 1999), preparation of country case studies (Mackay, 1998a;
Guerrero, 1999; Brushett, 1998; Hauge, 2001), preparation of a guide for
reviewing M&E training organizations (Adrien, 2001), and creation of an
ECB Web site: worldbank.org/evaluation/me/.

These efforts were successful in raising the profile of ECB within the
Bank and led to a number of requests for OED assistance in countries as
diverse as Honduras, Benin, and Poland.

The third and latest stage of the Bank's ECB work started around 1999
and reflected two significant developments. First was the debt-relief initiative for highly indebted poor countries. This initiative commenced in 1996,
and by 1999 specified (World Bank, 2000b) that eligible countries would
prepare a "Poverty Reduction Strategy Paper" (PRSP). PRSPs are intended
to map out the steps that the country proposes to take to ensure that the
savings from debt relief will be used in an effective manner to reduce
poverty. These papers have a strong focus on results (measurable reductions
in poverty), and they also encourage close attention to the relative cost-
effectiveness of alternative policies and programs for reducing poverty; this
is creating a strong demand for M&E.

The second development resulted from OED's efforts in recent years to
draw the attention of the Bank's board and senior management to deficien-
cies in the approach of the Bank's operational areas to M&E. At the end of
1999, Bank management responded by setting up a Bankwide task force
enquiring into the state of M&E in the Bank. The task force concluded that

M&E within the Bank and in borrower countries needs to be improved significantly, with much more emphasis on results (development outcomes) than on tracking inputs and deliverables.[2] The task force also recognized the need for ECB both within the Bank and in borrower countries.

An important mind-set change within the Bank was the recognition that high-quality M&E should be undertaken not just for Bank-funded projects but for all government activities of borrower countries. This change in thinking was stimulated by OED recommendations, and it acknowledges the support that M&E findings can provide to sound governance. As a result of the task force report, five additional developing countries were selected as pilots for country-based ECB in FY01, with additional countries being selected for later years. For FY01, the pilots in which ECB was initiated were Tanzania, Madagascar, the Kyrgyz Republic, the Philippines, and Romania. The ECB work in these countries is being managed by a core operational support unit within the Bank, which now has two full-time staff working on ECB, with advisory support from OED.

These three stages of Bank work on ECB over the past fourteen years reflect an evolution—a developmental process—from a situation in which only one OED staffer was working part-time on ECB to one in which a growing number of Bank country teams are interested in ECB and are actively supporting it. It would be premature to claim that ECB has yet been mainstreamed within the Bank, but it is increasingly being viewed as a legitimate activity.

The ECB Process: Lessons from Outreach Country Work

The Bank works on capacity building in many dimensions of sound governance, and this entails strengthening the skills and competencies of civil servants, parliamentarians, and representatives of civil society, as well as strengthening systems and functions within governments. These areas of governance include service delivery, policy analysis, ongoing agency management, budget systems, audit functions, and so on, and they encompass every possible type of government activity. This provides a substantive body of experience with capacity building generally—especially concerning what does and does not work (for example, World Bank, 1994; World Bank, 2000c).

This experience is consistent with and complemented by the Bank's ECB work with a growing number of countries, each with their own governance arrangements and opportunities and constraints on ECB.

Demand Is the Main Prerequisite. Success in capacity building, including ECB, requires an effective demand for it. Half-hearted government interest in any area of governance reform—possibly only in order to satisfy the expectations of international donors—would be unlikely to provide sufficient resources and the long-term commitment to achieve sustained change. ECB cannot be foisted on an unwilling government, and there is an awkward element of the chicken-and-egg problem here: a government is unlikely to be forthright in requesting help with ECB unless it is convinced of the merits of M&E, and a government may not be convinced of the merits of M&E if it hasn't devoted substantive efforts to M&E in the past. The way around this conundrum is to work to strengthen demand by raising awareness and providing education about what M&E has to offer to their specific situation. This advocacy role might seem unnecessary to professional evaluators convinced of the inherent value of M&E. But those of us working at ECB need to be able to persuade key decision makers that M&E is worth the effort; if we are unable to do this, we share the failure.

The Bank and other donors have sponsored a number of awareness-raising activities for ECB, such as regional seminars. With OED encouragement, Bank country teams have also approached governments directly to sound them out about their interest in ECB, and the influential position of the Bank has been helpful in persuading them of the benefits of this area of capacity building. It is usually not difficult to persuade the poorest countries about the need for ECB, as they are only too well aware of their many needs for capacity building. But it appears to be much more difficult to persuade middle-income countries in East Asia or Eastern Europe or Latin America about the merits of M&E. These countries are often fairly self-confident about their systems of governance and prefer to focus on the capacity-building priorities that they themselves identify rather than those suggested by external organizations such as the Bank.

Synergies with Other Capacity-Building Work. The ECB work of the Bank is usually not conducted as a stand-alone capacity-building effort but rather as part of larger governance efforts that encompass one or more of the governance issues listed earlier. The involvement of the Bank in a range of public sector reform activities enables close synergies between ECB activities and other capacity-building efforts. For example, when the Bank is helping a government reform its budget system, it is relatively easy to include an emphasis on the expected and actual performance of budget-funded government activities (as measured by M&E)—in other words, a focus on performance budgeting. But in the absence of broader work to reform a budget system, it is much harder to push a particular approach such as performance budgeting.

Having the support of the Bank's country team has proved invaluable in ECB work. The country teams are composed of Bank staffers, most of whom work with one or a handful of countries. These staffers include sector and thematic issue specialists, as well as experts in a range of governance issues. The country team has very good contacts with key decision makers in government and can use its influence to successfully advocate specific capacity-building activities. Working closely with the country team also provides an opportunity to increase their understanding about M&E and what it has to offer; this helps to build a community of understanding and support for M&E within the Bank.

Tailor ECB According to Country Circumstances. For the poorest and weakest-capacity countries, relatively simple M&E tools such as performance indicators might be the most cost-effective focus for the ECB work, at least in its early stages. This raises issues such as sequencing, timing, and the level of resources to be devoted to the ECB efforts by government and donors. There does not appear to be a unique or best approach to ECB, including how best to sequence it, as ECB is so dependent on country circumstances and priorities; this is one reason that ECB at the country level remains much more of an art than a science.

Conduct a Baseline Diagnosis. When working intensively in a country, OED conducts a detailed diagnosis of existing M&E activities, particularly of the capacities of government. This allows strengths and weaknesses to be pinpointed and helps identify the most promising opportunities for ECB. It also provides a baseline against which future progress in strengthening M&E can be assessed fairly. OED's detailed diagnostic guide (Mackay, 1999) provides a useful framework by focusing on the following key issues:

- Identify key ministries and stakeholders—the organizations within government that are important for performance management, such as the finance or planning ministries, the key sector ministries, and national audit office.
- Analyze the public sector environment, including incentives for managers and others, the existence of a service or performance culture, ethics, and the extent of corruption.
- Find out what influences government decision making and line management.
- Identify the influence of M&E, if any, on budget and line management decisions.
- Identify the M&E activities of government ministries and of NGOs, which relates to the existing *supply* of M&E, including the processes and systems for making that information available.
- Identify the M&E activities and roles of international donors such as the World Bank; in many countries, donors have been the most active players in M&E.
- What major public sector initiatives or reforms are under way or are planned: reforms in budgetary systems; intergovernmental fiscal relations, including decentralization; commercialization and private sector or NGO delivery of public services; performance agreements or contracts for senior officials; customer-client service standards; participation and the "voice" of civil society; anticorruption efforts; strengthening of accountability institutions; or capacity-building activities in areas such as the quality of civil service policy advice? If the government is also preparing a Poverty Reduction Strategy, there is likely to be some demand for strengthened M&E functions in the future.

- Map opportunities for ECB. A menu of ECB options can be assembled, based on the strength of demand and supply for M&E (Guerrero, 1999; Mackay, 1999).
- Prepare a realistic action plan.

ECB in Ghana: Laying the Groundwork

In 1999, the government of Ghana (GOG) approached OED for assistance in developing M&E capacities. With the active involvement of the country team and other parts of the Bank, OED undertook two missions that worked closely with senior GOG officials to prepare a diagnosis of M&E capacities and to draft an action plan (World Bank, 2000a). A diagnostic report was presented at two brainstorming workshops for officials and at a workshop for civil society representatives (Mackay and Gariba, 2000).

As a result, GOG decided in May 2000 on an action plan with several key priorities and requested continued Bank support. As a first step, OED and the Bank's training arm jointly arranged provision of trainer-training in evaluation for staff of the main training organization in Ghana. OED also commissioned a review of the evaluation training capacities of key Ghanaian organizations (Adrien, 2001) to identify their strengths and weaknesses and thus help determine GOG's capacity-building priorities for them.

A Bank "Public Financial Management Reform Project" is currently in preparation. Inter alia, this project would provide support for Ghana's ECB efforts and would also help to strengthen the participation of civil society, universities, think-tanks, and parliament in monitoring and assessing public sector performance.

ECB Action Plans. A draft action plan, preferably one prepared by the government, should provide a focus for debate and discussion within the country and with other donors that might be prepared to support ECB. The discussion should be on how and where to build awareness and demand; on which types of M&E tools and techniques to focus; how to broaden and deepen evaluation skills; whether to focus on ECB at the national level or only for specific sectors or major projects; what types of information infrastructure to strengthen; what types of support or other involvement could be obtained from donors; and timelines, sequencing, and speed of implementation.

Key components of an action plan might focus on

- The role of M&E advocates (or influential champions) within government
- M&E functions within sector ministries
- Coordinating roles of finance and planning ministries
- Strengthening of the national statistics office
- Involvement of civil society, including NGOs, universities, research institutes, and so on

- Training in M&E, including trainer-training for staff of universities or civil service colleges
- The nature and extent of support from donors

To assist in the preparation of ECB action plans, OED has developed a checklist of eleven criteria for what it regards as good-quality country-level ECB:

1. Based on a formal country diagnosis and a clear action plan?
2. Form part of a public sector management reform program?
3. Promote a results orientation and a poverty reduction and growth focus?
4. Connect oversight of public expenditures at central, sector, and regional levels?
5. Involve civil society, NGOs, private sector?
6. Support parallel initiatives by other development assistance agencies?
7. Develop and implement a customized training program for ECB?
8. Establish linkages with financial management and accountability programs?
9. Develop linkages with statistical system improvements?
10. Establish linkages with research initiatives?
11. Contribute to improved M&E for country or sector assistance strategies and donor-financed projects?

ECB Results Chain. Figure 5.1 shows the desired "results chain" for country-based ECB. Some suggested performance indicators for each stage in the results chain of a country undertaking ECB are shown in Table 5.1. It will be evident from the discussion so far that preparation of a detailed diagnosis and a draft action plan are only the first steps for pursuing ECB. As indicated also in Figure 5.1, continuing efforts will be needed to build awareness and to create or strengthen demand for M&E, focusing partly on government, partly on civil society, and perhaps pursuing a collegiate approach among a number of stakeholders in government, civil society, and the donor community. These demand-side efforts will need to be balanced by capacity building on the supply side, via training and development of ministry systems and procedures for M&E. Pursued jointly, these demand and supply-side efforts would be intended to lead to the production of a greater quantity and better quality of monitoring information and evaluation findings. Of course, this in itself is not the end of the story. The next step in the desired results chain is utilization; without this, the ECB efforts will have failed. Utilization can be achieved if M&E actively supports accountability, resource allocation decisions, and management via learning. And if utilization is achieved, M&E would be more likely to be a sustainable and enduring function of government. Finally, it is expected and certainly hoped that

**Table 5.1. Some Suggested Performance Indicators for
Bank's Country-Level ECB**

Results Area	Suggested Performance Indicators
Outcomes	• M&E findings are used in budget decision making, in sectoral strategy making, and in line management decisions • M&E findings are used by media, in parliamentary debates, and in NGO submissions to government • Government structures and processes have been realigned to commission M&E findings and to feed them into budget processes and into ministries' planning and management processes
Outputs	• Greater quantity and better quality of monitoring information and evaluation findings • Formal M&E framework is established by government • Number of officials who undertake M&E training • Number of officials working on M&E (full-time equivalents) • Number of evaluations or reviews conducted
Activities	• Extent to which civil society is involved in assessing government performance • Bank makes a loan or a grant to government for the purpose of supporting its ECB • Baseline ECB diagnosis conducted • M&E training and trainer-training offered • In-country seminars provided for senior officials and civil society representatives to build awareness and stregthen demand for M&E

utilization of M&E findings will improve government performance and thus enhance its effectiveness in reducing poverty.

Mainstreaming and Selectivity. One definition of success for OED in its advocacy of ECB within the Bank is that all Bank country teams come to view ECB as a worthwhile and important activity for the countries with which they work. This situation would represent the mainstreaming of ECB within the Bank.

A trade-off that OED has to make in deciding what level of ECB support to provide to any one country is between mainstreaming and selectivity. Although its objective is to mainstream ECB for all developing countries, OED only has sufficient resources to work in-depth on a handful. So a small number of countries have been selected where the potential exists for building "good-practice" demonstration pilots that will be persuasive to other countries and to other Bank country teams. For other countries, OED encourages country team staffers to take responsibility for ECB, with OED assistance limited to provision of resource materials and comments on ECB diagnoses and other relatively low-intensity support, such as identification of good-practice approaches, available training courses, and suitable consultants.

Figure 5.1. Results Chain for Country-Based ECB

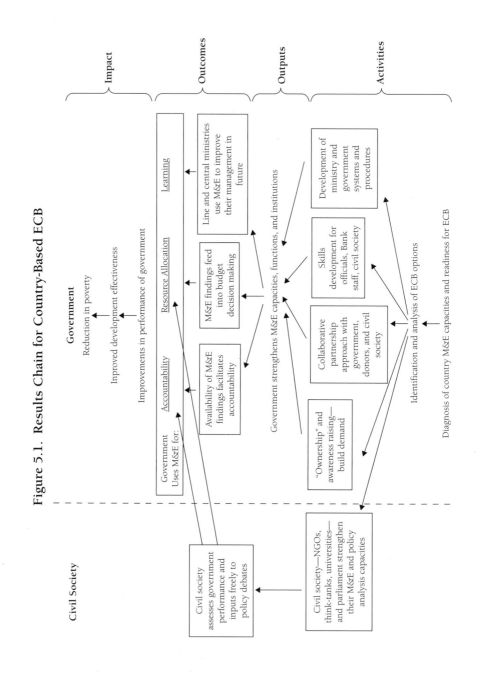

This latter approach relies on the *capacity-building* expertise of Bank country staff, and it thus reflects a view that evaluation expertise is *not* a prerequisite for those managing ECB activities. Such expertise is clearly necessary for particular ECB activities, such as provision of in-country training, but these skills can be hired from consultants and universities.

Although the Bank does not offer formal training in ECB to its staff, a number of case studies have been prepared and disseminated widely, brown-bag lunch seminars on topical ECB issues are offered from time to time, and there have been several longer seminars on ECB in recent years.

OED experience over the past fourteen years is that it has often been easier to persuade developing country governments about the need for ECB than it has been to persuade Bank staff. In the absence of the active support of the Bank team, OED would be likely to restrict its response to any government request for ECB assistance to the provision of resource materials. OED also has an evaluation help desk that provides government officials, academics, NGOs, and others with copies of published Bank evaluations and references to non-Bank material such as evaluation manuals, texts, and the "Guiding Principles for Evaluators" (American Evaluation Association, 1994).

Civil Society. Until the last couple of years, the Bank's ECB work was focused on governments. But there is now an increasing emphasis on the role of civil society (for example, Mackay and Gariba, 2000; Songco, 2001). This partly reflects the growing recognition of the desirable role of civil society in decisions about national priorities. It also reflects the growing realization that although governments are part of the solution to poverty in developing countries, they can also be part of the problem.

Civil society can play an important role in M&E in at least four ways: (1) by inputting beneficiary feedback on government service delivery; (2) as producers of analysis and reviews of government performance; (3) by providing independent scrutiny of monitoring information and evaluation findings produced by governments; and (4) as users of M&E (Mackay, 2001). Civil society can thus be a complement and a substitute to governments in the conduct of M&E; at the very least, civil society can provide some element of quality assurance and a second opinion on M&E findings. One promising development in the past several years has been the growth of national associations of professional evaluators in African countries such as Kenya, Niger, and Rwanda (see, for example, Segone, forthcoming).

Assessment of the Bank's ECB Work

There has not yet been a thorough evaluation of the Bank's ECB work. But a 1994 task force report (World Bank, 1994) identified a number of lessons concerning what does or does not work when attempting ECB, as OED also did at that time (Operations Evaluation Department, 1994). A number of seminars have also identified ECB lessons (for example, Inter-American Development Bank (IDB) and Organisation for Economic Co-operation and Development (OECD), 1994; Central American Evaluation Association, International Fund for Agricultural Development and IDB, 1994; IDB and Colombian National Planning Department, 1997; Mackay, 1998b; African Development Bank and World Bank, 1999; Malik and Roth, 2000; African Development Bank, Development Bank of South Africa and World Bank, 2001). And OED plans to report to the Bank's board in mid-2002 on progress with the current round of ECB efforts. The main lessons are discussed in the next section.

If the Bank's work is assessed partly in terms of the level of demand for ECB, it is notable that substantive demand has recently been strengthened or created in a number of Bank country teams and in governments. Bank loans or grants for ECB have been agreed to or are under preparation for Honduras, Poland, Ghana, Brazil, Uganda, Guinea, Niger, and Romania. And other governments that have asked for assistance with ECB (some of which have already agreed to an ECB diagnosis being conducted) include Tanzania, Madagascar, Egypt, Malawi, and Lesotho. These efforts are all at fairly early stages and can be viewed very much as "work in progress." The Bank understands that ECB at the country level is a long-term endeavor, requiring sustained efforts by the government and by donors such as the Bank if the work is to be successful.

In assessing the level of acceptance of ECB as a worthwhile activity, it is evident that the Bank is increasingly committed to ECB and that it is being accorded a reasonably high priority. Although the five country "pilots" recently nominated by Bank management are indeed pilots, the implication is not that the work would be terminated if progress is somehow judged inadequate. Instead, the pilots are more in the nature of action-learning opportunities, so that the Bank's approach to ECB can be fine-tuned in light of the additional experience the pilots will provide. The pressures to support the poorest countries in their national decision making, including the regular preparation of Poverty Reduction Strategies, puts a premium on trying to ensure that ECB becomes a commonplace or even a standard activity in these countries. How quickly this can be done is unclear.

To help achieve this, it is important to develop a few good demonstration countries to provide models that can be pointed to as examples of "success." The Bank's new pilot countries might fill this role, as might the several countries with which OED commenced its ECB in the past several years, especially Uganda, Ghana, and the Kyrgyz Republic. Other developing countries that have laid the groundwork for good M&E systems via "home-grown" initiatives, such as Chile (Marcel, 1998), Brazil (Brazilian Ministry of Planning, 2001), and possibly Colombia (World Bank, 1997b), also have considerable potential to be influential in persuading others about the feasibility and value of ECB.

Lessons from This Case Example

One key lesson is the need for patience and persistence in ECB efforts. ECB at the whole-of-government level is not a quick fix, and neither has it proved quick to build acceptance of the importance of ECB within the Bank. Awareness and demand have to be cultivated carefully, and this is where a powerful and influential champion has a pivotal role to play. Within the Bank, that champion has been OED, with persistent pressure from its vice president. ECB efforts will fail unless real demand exists or can be intentionally created, especially by ensuring that powerful incentives are in place to do and to use M&E. It is not sufficient to issue an edict that M&E are important and should be done; this is likely to produce only lip service and is certainly unlikely to achieve the conduct and utilization of high-quality evaluation. Such efforts at top-down compliance can, unless accompanied by a range of other actions, easily lead to ritual compliance or even active resistance. This search and cultivation of allies is seen clearly in the CDC case study.

The building of demand needs to be done in an opportunistic manner; there are often sympathetic "fellow travelers" in a ministry or government who see the merit of M&E and who are willing to support ECB efforts. Although finding and cultivating these allies takes time and care, their tangible and moral support can be invaluable to those of us working full-time on ECB. Spearheading any reform of this nature can be a very lonely business, and their support can be very helpful in establishing connections with activities related to ECB, such as statistical capacity building.

For country-based ECB, it is important to tailor the work according to country circumstances; a cookie-cutter or supply-driven approach would be ineffective. For the poorest countries in particular, low-tech M&E tools are most likely to be relevant, but even then only if there are synergistic opportunities to use M&E arising from particular types of public sector reform.

The focus, speed, and sequencing of ECB depend very much on the starting point (the country's strengths and weaknesses), on national priorities, and on country judgments about the cost-effectiveness of various M&E tools. This tailoring of ECB to the needs and priorities of each country underscores the desirability of conducting a baseline diagnosis of M&E activities for identifying ECB opportunities. This is also an argument for a gradual and incremental approach to country-level ECB, recognizing that it is a long-haul effort to build and sustain both demand and supply.

A Conceptual Definition of ECB. By now the Bank's approach to ECB should be reasonably clear to the reader. Someone skimming this volume quickly might be tempted to skip over this chapter on the World Bank's experience, perceiving it as too specialized, esoteric, and separate from the mainstream ECB issues facing organizations in developed countries. That would be a mistake. Although ECB work in developing countries could be viewed as being at one end of the ECB spectrum, it is precisely its large, whole-of-government scale and the diversity of environments in which it is being attempted that make its lessons so valuable elsewhere.

The applicability of the Bank's work on ECB is illustrated by its implications for definitions of ECB. The conceptual definition proposed in this volume contains a number of dimensions. The Bank's approach to ECB strongly confirms a number of these, but it differs in several respects.

One key area of strong congruence is the objective of achieving an *ongoing, enduring, and sustainable state of affairs* where evaluation is utilized. Thus the desired situation is one in which a senior executive, middle manager, or line staffer would display the attitude that "we need evaluation—of course it should be done" rather than the more common mind-set: "Why on earth would we want to do an evaluation?" The sustainability dimension is crucial, and Bank experience with ECB and many other areas of capacity building is that demand has to be strong, both for a process of change and for a different way of doing business to be enduring. Thus a conscious effort to strengthen the demand for evaluation must be an important part of the ECB process.

Another area of clear agreement is the need for ECB to involve a *guided* process. ECB does not just happen on its own; it needs clear guidance and ongoing support. This support should include a strong champion who is both willing and able to push hard for ECB to happen and to keep pushing hard until it has become embedded in the corporate culture. It should also include support such as the provision to line units within the organization of easily understandable evaluation findings and recommended action items. This comes back to the issue of buy-in and demand.

Nor is it realistic to start with a blueprint design for ECB and expect to adhere to it rigidly throughout this process. Good-quality ECB is opportunistic and reacts quickly to changing circumstances. Again, having a senior champion who is closely attuned to emerging corporate priorities has been proved invaluable to a range of capacity-building efforts.

An emphasis on *utilization* is another important dimension of the ECB definition. This is the bottom-line measure of ECB success, and utilization reflects the existence of demand for evaluation. For ECB to be worthwhile, there should be reasonable prospects for evaluation utilization at the end of the process unless one is prepared to argue to the organization's CEO that knowledge has its own value; this is likely to be a hard sell.

But there are two important and related areas where the approach to ECB in this chapter differs from that found in the introduction to this volume. Perhaps surprisingly, these are the stated focus on *quality* and on *evaluation*. The Bank's approach to ECB encompasses a broad array of M&E tools, not just program evaluation. And although it is always legitimate to emphasize high-quality work (who would disagree with this "motherhood" goal?), this might not be appropriate in a number of situations. It is most starkly evident in the poorest developing countries where there is often a severe shortage of quality data, of qualified evaluators, and of the funding needed to conduct rigorous program evaluations. Such evaluations are feasible but require special data collection, and often also that highly paid, international experts be contracted. There is an issue here of cost-effectiveness for the immediate purpose at hand, which revolves around what performance issues need to be measured and why. But there is also a strategic issue relating to ECB and to the objective of building a performance culture: what types of evaluative (M&E) activity—rigorous program evaluation, rapid review, performance indicators—will yield a cost-effective, immediate, and strong pay-off in demonstrating the merits of M&E? In some circumstances, a rigorous program evaluation might fit the bill. In others it might be that the existence of agency performance indicators will lead to demands for the application of more rigorous evaluative tools to answer the key causality questions, as is happening in the U.S. federal government with the GPRA initiative (Newcomer and Scheirer, 2001).

The American experience in particular poses an interesting and important series of ECB questions. Why did the evaluation hey-day in the federal government during the 1960s and 1970s come to an end? To what extent had a performance culture and strong evaluative skills been built within the civil service? And do these existing skills provide a springboard for more intensive program evaluation activities within the government? The answers to these questions lie outside the scope of this chapter but would help us all understand better the nature of opportunities and constraints on ECB.

Notes

1. The close support and encouragement of my manager, Osvaldo Feinstein, in the Bank's ECB work is gratefully acknowledged.
2. The task force also concluded that the weaknesses in M&E resulted from three causes: (1) poor incentives for Bank operational areas and for borrower countries to conduct and utilize M&E; (2) for these two groups, diffused and unclear accountabilities as to who has what responsibilities for M&E; (3) weak capacities within these two groups to undertake M&E.

References

Adrien, M-H. "Guide to Conducting Reviews of Organizations Supplying M&E Training." Draft report prepared for the World Bank (mimeo), 2001.

African Development Bank and OED. *Evaluation Capacity Development in Africa: Selected Proceedings from a Seminar in Abidjan*. Washington, D.C.: The African Development Bank and The World Bank, 1999.

African Development Bank, Development Bank of South Africa and World Bank. *Proceedings of a Regional Seminar on Monitoring and Evaluation Capacity Development in Africa*. Abidjan, Côte d'Ivoire: African Development Bank, 2001.

American Evaluation Association. "Guiding Principles for Evaluators" (mimeo), 1994.

Baker, J. L. *Evaluating the Impact of Development Projects on Poverty: A Handbook for Practitioners*. Washington, D.C.: World Bank, 2000.

Brazilian Ministry of Planning (Ministerio do Planejamento, Orcamento e Gestao), *Plano Plurianual—PPA: 2000–2003. Relatorio Anual de Avaliacao—Exercicio 2000*. Brasilia, Brazil, 2001.

Brushett, S. *Zimbabwe: Issues and Opportunities*. OED Working Paper No. 2. Washington, D.C.: World Bank, 1998.

Central American Evaluation Association, International Fund for Agricultural

Development and Inter-American Development Bank. *First Evaluation Seminar for Central America, Panama & The Dominican Republic*. Washington, D.C.: Central American Evaluation Association, 1994.

Gittinger, J. P. *Economic Analysis of Agricultural Projects*. Baltimore: Johns Hopkins University Press, 1982.

Guerrero, O. P. *Comparative Insights from Colombia, China and Indonesia*. OED Working Paper No. 5. Washington, D.C.: World Bank, 1999.

Hauge, A. "Strengthening Capacity for Monitoring and Evaluation in Uganda: A Results Based Management Perspective." OED Working Paper No. 8. Washington, D.C.: World Bank, 2001.

Inter-American Development Bank (IDB) and Colombian National Planning Department. *South American Meeting on Results-Based Evaluation and Control of Public Management*. Washington, D.C.: Inter-American Development Bank, 1997.

Inter-American Development Bank (IDB) and Organisation for Economic Co-operation and Development (OECD). Regional Seminar on Monitoring and Evaluation in Latin America and the Caribbean: Strengthening Evaluation Capabilities for Sustainable Development. Paris: Inter-American Development Bank, 1994.

Mackay, K. "The Development of Australia's Evaluation System." OED Working Paper No. 4. Washington, D.C.: World Bank, 1998a.

Mackay, K. (ed.) *Public Sector Performance: The Critical Role of Evaluation*. Washington, D.C.: World Bank, 1998b.

Mackay, K. "Evaluation Capacity Development: A Diagnostic Guide and Action Framework." OED Working Paper No. 6. Washington, D.C.: World Bank, 1999.

Mackay, K. "New Trends of Evaluation in Public Policy Reform and Governance." In African Development Bank, Development Bank of South Africa and World Bank, *Proceedings of a Regional Seminar on Monitoring and Evaluation Capacity Development in Africa*. Abidjan, Côte d'Ivoire: African Development Bank, 2001.

Mackay, K., and Gariba, S. (eds.). *The Role of Civil Society in Assessing Public Sector Performance in Ghana: Proceedings of a Workshop*. Washington, D.C.: OED/World Bank, 2000.

Malik, K., and Roth, C. *Evaluation Capacity Development in Asia: Selected Proceedings from the International Conference, Beijing, October 1999*. New York: UNDP (United Nations Development Program), Chinese National Center for Science and Technology Evaluation, and the World Bank, 2000.

Marcel, M. "Lessons from Chile." In K. Mackay (ed.), *Public Sector Performance: The Critical Role of Evaluation*. Washington, D.C.: World Bank, 1998.

Newcomer, K. E., and Scheirer, M. A. *Using Evaluation to Support Performance Management: A Guide for Federal Executives*. Arlington, Va.: PricewaterhouseCoopers, 2001.

Operations Evaluation Department. *Building Evaluation Capacity*, OED Lessons & Practices No. 4. Washington, D.C.: World Bank, 1994.

Operations Evaluation Department. *Assessing Development Effectiveness: Evaluation in the World Bank and the International Finance Corporation*. Washington, D.C.: World Bank, 1998.

Picciotto, R. "The New Challenge of Evaluation Capacity Development." In *Evaluation Cooperation Group Newsletter*, 1999, *1*(1), 1–2.

Picciotto, R. "Change at the World Bank." Paper presented at a meeting of the 1818 H Society, Harrogate, United Kingdom, 2001.

Segone, M. "Sustainable Monitoring & Evaluation Capacity Development in Africa: The Case of the Nigerian Monitoring & Evaluation Network." In African Development Bank, Development Bank of South Africa and World Bank, *Proceedings of a Regional Seminar on Monitoring and Evaluation Capacity Development in Africa*. Abidjan, Côte d'Ivoire: African Development Bank, forthcoming.

Songco, D. "Accountability to the Poor: Experiences in Civil Engagement in Public Expenditure Management." Report prepared for the World Bank (mimeo), 2001.

Squire, L., and Van der Tak, H. *The Economic Analysis of Projects.* Baltimore: Johns Hopkins University Press, 1975.

World Bank. "Evaluation Capacity Development." Report of the Task Force (mimeo), 1994.

World Bank. *The State in a Changing World: World Development Report, 1997.* Washington, D.C.: World Bank, 1997a.

World Bank. *Colombia: Paving the Way for a Results-Oriented Public Sector.* Washington, D.C.: World Bank, 1997b.

World Bank. "Monitoring and Evaluation Capacities in Ghana: A Diagnosis and Proposed Action Plan." Report prepared for the Government of Ghana. World Bank, 2000a.

World Bank. *Partners in Transforming Development: New Approaches to Developing Country-Owned Poverty Reduction Strategies.* Washington, D.C.: World Bank, 2000b.

World Bank. *Reforming Public Institutions and Strengthening Governance: A World Bank Strategy.* Washington, D.C.: World Bank, 2000c.

KEITH MACKAY is ECB coordinator, World Bank, Washington, D.C.

6

The authors provide analysis, reflection, and integration of the four studies in this chapter on themes across the cases. This serves to ground their conceptual definition of ECB with examples.

Summary and Analysis of the Case Studies: Themes Across the Cases

Michael Baizerman, Donald W. Compton, Stacey Hueftle Stockdill

In this journal, case studies are included so that we can compare ECB work, so accomplished practitioners can have an opportunity to reflect on their day-to-day practice, and readers can more easily touch and see ECB as a type of everyday organizational work. We summarize and analyze the four case studies, first presenting our findings in a matrix and then discussing major themes in the context of our conceptual definition of ECB.

Main Themes in the Case Studies

The four case studies were analyzed using two dimensions. The first evolved from the guidelines authors were given for writing the case studies. Authors were asked to write their case study using four broad headings: (1) the context of their case, (2) their ECB story, (3) how ECB was assessed, and (4) what was learned about ECB. As we reviewed the four case studies, these headings became four questions:

What is the context of the ECB story?
What is the ECB story?
How was ECB assessment done?
What was learned?

In the analysis, we added the three structural elements of ECB. Recall that they are the overall ECB process, actual ECB practices, and ECB occupational orientation and practitioner role. What resulted is a 3 × 4 matrix (see Table 6.1). It is presented to facilitate your analysis and reflection on

Table 6.1. Main Themes in the Case Studies

	Context of the ECB Story	The ECB Story	How ECB Assessment Was Done	What Was Learned
Overall Process	• Context means the shape of ECB in relation to the organization's history, external environments, and type. • Without context, the ECB story makes little sense, suggesting that whether and how ECB is done is time- and place-specific. • Understanding the history of the organization or program, as well as its organizational culture and structure, are crucial for understanding ECB.	• ECB is not a program evaluation process. • There is an ECB process, but very few stories are told or written about it. • The case studies' narrative structure gives coherence to the ECB process, which may be invisible. • There was no consistent language or discourse used to describe the ECB process. • There is more in the case studies about the overall process than about actual ECB practices.	• A formal assessment of ECB was done in one case; in others, the ECB process was assessed by the ECB practitioners and their colleagues as part of their reflective and political practice.	• There is an identifiable overall ECB process that is distinguishable from evaluation practice and work. • There is no standard ECB language or discourse outside of international work. • ECB is understood using very few root metaphors. • The ECB process is never-ending.
Actual Practices	• How ECB was carried out depended on the organizational contexts (structure, culture, roles, and skills) and ever-changing situations.	• ECB work is different from program evaluation work. • Narratives can be interpreted as a seeking of confirmation of the legitimacy and value of ECB work. • ECB practice means working simultaneously in several orientations: co-creating and co-sustaining evaluation and its uses, while at the same time working to prevent the loss of gains. • Not much detail was given in the case studies regarding actual ECB practices.	• Monitoring the organizational environment and actions of others for evidence that ECB was working (for example, invited to a high-level meeting, resources allocated to the effort, a smiley face put on the practitioner's desk) increased demand for evaluation and training.	• There is a wide variety of practices reported; very few seem unique to ECB practice. • Practices must be inclusive and are inherently and intentionally political. • There are identifiable time and work phases, the validity of which are yet to be proven. • Practices are difficult to name, and there is little description of how these are carried out; more research is needed. • Most ECB practices are collegial rather than done alone, thus making the literature of small groups, coalitions, and collaborations relevant. • ECB is far easier for an internal ECB practitioner.

Occupational Orientation and Practitioner Role	• *Context* means the changing space-time horizons of what is important to pay attention to. • ECB orientation gives prominence and importance to some and not other aspects of organizational context and ever-changing situations. • Ever-changing organizational context tells the ECB practitioner what to pay attention to. • ECB practice is always bifocal and dual-vision: both forest and trees, here (for example, central office) and there (for example, field office in Cuba, Cancer Control Department), now and in the future. • ECB orientation joins these space-time horizons to changing contexts of what is relevant and important.	• Occupational orientation and practitioner role are clearly distinguishable from program evaluation practice and work. • Authors wrote from a discernible stance about themselves as ECB practitioners and the roles they took on in their ECB work. • ECB work is reflective practice, requiring self-awareness, learning from the work, and changing to meet always-emergent situations. • ECB work is hard but achievable, if not always sustainable. • How the work was carried out related to authors' professional identification and training. • The authors guided and facilitated rather than controlled the ECB process. • ECB work is carried out primarily in groups and rarely alone. • Authors tell stories of frustrations. • Practitioners have relatively little control of the ECB process because external realities always intrude. • ECB practitioners work within and across ever-changing organizational worlds. • "Practice wisdom," rules of thumb, and philosophy guide practitioners more than ECB theory.	• Self-reflective practitioner • Reading of the environment and ongoing crafting of one's role in response.	• ECB and program evaluation are distinct yet complementary occupational orientations with related, distinct, yet complementary practitioner roles. • Authors show identifiable ECB occupational orientations, and these were closely linked to how they went about the work. • Other occupational orientations included an "outwardness" toward the organization and its environments and potential collaborations; others were reading the organization and the work as political, change-oriented, long term, and as always emergent. • ECB work is largely derived from other practices and is brought together for this process, which is unique in its specifics. • ECB work is more craft than art or science.

the cases, to encourage you to write and publish your ECB work, and to serve as a beginning framework for understanding the everyday realities of actual ECB practice.

The matrix provides a detailed account of what was learned from the case studies about ECB. What was learned, in general, is obvious and important: *an identifiable and reportable ECB process exists.* Because this ECB process has only recently been made explicit, it remains relatively nonspecific, with somewhat unclear practices and with little systematic assessment. Because there are as yet no "thick descriptions" of ECB work—detailed stories of ECB practices in their immediacy, complexity, and emergence—it is impossible to get at the subtleties, the everyday ordinariness and politics of ECB practice— its art and craft. It is also impossible to get at the details of the ECB occupational orientation and practitioner role—the skills, the personal theorizing (for example, Ross, Cornett, and McCutcheon, 1992), the "intuition" (for example, Hogarth, 2001), and what it means to work as a "reflective practitioner" (Schön, 1983). Nomothetic understanding of general practices awaits more idiographic studies of ECB practitioners and their work. The science of ECB is newly born.

We also learned from the case studies that ECB work is highly context-dependent; its content and shape are formed by practitioner judgment and based in site realities. Actual ECB is shown to be within an orientation to organizational change and development. Practitioners take on bifocal or dual vision, attending to both evaluation studies and their use and to organizational structure, culture, and process, which makes these studies and their use possible. ECB work can be undertaken effectively by several professions; it requires some but not full expert knowledge of program evaluation processes and practices. There is as yet no consensus, except in international work, on the details of the overall ECB process, of actual ECB practices, or the occupational orientation and practitioner roles.

Grounding the Conceptual Definition

The case studies can also be read using the eleven elements of our conceptual definition of ECB. Next we return to these same elements and show examples of each, taken from the case studies. Recall the conceptual definition of ECB: a context-dependent, intentional action system of guided processes and practices for bringing about and sustaining a state of affairs in which quality program evaluation and its appropriate uses are ordinary and ongoing practices within and/or between one or more organizations/programs/sites.

The first of the eleven elements is that ECB is *context-dependent.* In the four case studies, the strategies used and the day-to-day ECB work fit into the structure, culture, and ways of working specific to that setting. For example, the organizational structure, scientific culture, and work ways of CDC were used to craft the series of meetings that led to publications, to policy, and to new ways of integrating evaluation work into that federal agency. In their details, each case study shows concrete, specific differences—the realities of the organizational context of ECB.

The second element is that ECB is an *intentional action system* and not the result of random acts, luck, or simple hard work. Basic to the element are a vision, a more or less clear goal, and plans; also basic is purposive, attentive, and reflective work with others, in order to create and sustain ways of ensuring that evaluation studies and their uses continue to be carried out in the organization. At the ACS, a high demand for evaluation studies, coupled with few resources, led the evaluator to conceive of and carry out ECB work—always with others, inside and outside that voluntary agency. The World Bank is always "intentional" in its work around ECB, and the school district example shows the evaluator's intentional efforts to build useful and practical evaluation presence at the district and building levels.

ECB is a *guided process,* typically because the evaluation staff has limited authority and power outside their own unit. This leads to the necessity of working with others in co-created alliances, relationships, and actions. The CDC and ACS cases illustrate this well, in that both are oriented to guiding processes that change the centrality and utility of the evaluation function within their agencies. One indicator is the number of meetings the ECB practitioners attend with their colleagues to work jointly on evaluation topics.

It is easy to see the fourth element: ECB as a *process* rather than an end. The school district, CDC, and ACS case studies show vividly the ongoing, process nature of ECB work: meetings, meetings, meetings, with the work never completed "once and for all." In the school district case, multiple processes at the building and district levels had to be guided. At the ACS, there was work at the national home office, in the regional offices, and in local units.

If ECB is a process, then the ordinary, day-to-day work constituting ECB are its practices. At the ACS and the CDC, the everyday work included meetings with colleagues inside and outside the organizations (for example, to design and carry out specific evaluation studies, to write contracts to complete these studies, to plan staff training in evaluation practice, to create an evaluation unit Web site). Most explicit is the school district example, where the everyday, ordinary work necessary to carry out evaluation, as well as the ordinary work necessary to build and sustain the organizational supports for these studies, was made difficult, often seemingly impossible, by the lack of staff, funds, and equipment.

The sixth element is bringing about and sustaining those conditions that allow, invite, facilitate, support, and otherwise make mundane the carrying out of evaluation studies and their uses. This is seen most clearly in the ACS and school district cases, in which intentional effort was given to co-creating the conditions—the "state of affairs"—where evaluation studies would be requested and used. By the very nature of the four organizations, indeed in these times and in most complex organizations, ECB is about continuously sustaining what has been achieved, never knowing for sure whether the evaluation unit (or function) will be minimized, closed, or even expanded. The ACS case shows this well, with the profound changes brought about by new forms of organizational structure, decision-making patterns, the role of volunteers, and the like.

The "state of affairs" is a force that "right now" is supportive (or not) of evaluation work. It is always changing, requiring continuous intentional work to sustain. The school district and ACS case studies show this on the level of ECB and on the level of particular evaluation studies and their uses. For example, budget freezes and cuts dramatically changed the state of affairs at both, with evaluation work circumscribed. ECB is political work too, and a state of affairs is also a temporal condition of authority, power, and resources—obviously. Evaluation is rarely a powerful player in most organizations and is rarely "at the table" when major organizational, even program decisions, are made. This is seen again in the ACS case, while in the school district case there was access to decision makers but not sufficient resources to make real the evaluation's full potential contribution to the school and building staff and school district leaders.

The eighth element is that ECB can be *within or between* organizations, as well as programs, communities, and other social formations. At the ACS, it is within a nationwide organization and at three levels; at the World Bank it is within a nation, within a governmental ministry and its units, and between ministries. In the school district, ECB was on the district and school levels, as were the evaluation studies. At the CDC, ECB was both centerwide and within centers.

Quality program evaluation, element nine, refers to the expert and professional practice of evaluation, following the Joint Committee's standards (Joint Committee on Standards for Education Evaluation, 1994). In the school district and ACS examples, evaluation studies were carried out explicitly within these terms. The World Bank ECB professionals support such standards for in-country work, although this may be hard to ensure, given local expertise, political forces, and other resources. At the CDC, the story was about making evaluation central rather than about doing evaluation studies, but given their professional culture, it is highly likely that all their studies will meet norms of professional, quality work.

The tenth element covers the *appropriate uses* of evaluation studies, suggesting that ECB include both the completion of studies and their appropriate uses. The World Bank encourages practical use, as does the CDC. The school district case is about the practical use of studies on both district and building levels, with recognition of the difficulties in making use an ordinary part of the evaluation and ECB processes—due to lack of expertise, timing of decisions, how evaluation reports are written, and politics.

Finally, ECB is constituted by the *ordinary practices* of everyday, mundane work in which evaluation studies are conceived, designed, carried out, analyzed, and used in regular organizational work. This was the goal in the ACS study but one only partially realized. Although the World Bank case study tells about this, it is generally more as a goal than as a reality in consultative governmental practice.

Taken together, these eleven elements of our conceptual definition of ECB show at a beginning level this intentional work to bring about and sustain the routine practice of quality program evaluation and its uses. Building on these case studies, our analysis and discussion of them and on the ECB-related literature, we provide next a practical checklist for assessing ECB at an organization and a framework for developing the practice and scholarship of ECB—our proposed new direction.

References

Hogarth, R. *Educating Intuition.* Chicago: University of Chicago Press, 2001.
Joint Committee on Standards for Education Evaluation. *The Program Evaluation Standards.* (2nd ed.) Thousand Oaks, Calif.: Sage, 1994.
Mabry, L. (ed.). "Evaluation and the Postmodern Dilemma." In *Advances in Program Evaluation,* no. 3. Greenwich, Conn.: JAI Press, 1997.
Ross, E., Cornett, J., and McCutcheon, G. (eds.). *Teacher Personal Theorizing: Connecting Curriculum Practice, Theory and Research.* Albany, N.Y.: State University of New York Press, 1992.
Schön, D. A. *The Reflective Practitioner.* New York: Basic Books, 1983.

MICHAEL BAIZERMAN *is a professor in the School of Social Work and adjunct professor in the College of Education and Human Development and in the School of Public Health at the University of Minnesota, St. Paul.*

DONALD W. COMPTON *is director of the Division Evaluation Services, American Cancer Society, National Home Office, Atlanta.*

STACEY HUEFTLE STOCKDILL *is founder and CEO of EnSearch, Inc., a specialized evaluation firm in St. Paul, Minnesota.*

*The authors conclude this volume by framing the
definitions, literature review, and case studies as
practical and usable ECB indicators; a practical checklist
for site assessment is included. The volume concludes
with a reflection on its title.*

New Directions for ECB

*Michael Baizerman, Donald W. Compton,
Stacey Hueftle Stockdill*

This volume represents a beginning mapping of ECB as a process, an occupational orientation, and a practice—part art, part craft, and part science. From a review of the ECB literature in the international context, ECB practice, and related non-ECB literature, we have come to understand that ECB processes and practices are different from, yet show a resemblance to, program evaluation processes and practices.

Often theoretical work strives for a definition of a construct. In writing this journal issue, we found that we had to begin with a conceptual definition, as we found ourselves in old paradigms regarding what the words *evaluation, capacity,* and *building* meant. The ECB literature from the international arena and from practice forced us to view the words anew. So the *conceptual definition* became: ECB is a context-dependent, intentional action system of guided processes and practices for bringing about and sustaining a state of affairs in which quality program evaluation and its appropriate uses are ordinary and ongoing practices within and/or between one or more organizations/programs/sites.

And it evolved to this practical, usable, and flexible *working definition:* ECB is the intentional work to continuously create and sustain overall organizational processes that make quality evaluation and its uses routine.

Much work remains to further ECB. In this last chapter, we begin that work by moving the new direction for ECB toward a framework to guide practice and scholarly reflection. We present three sections: (1) practical indicators for assessing ECB in an organization, (2) a framework for ECB practice and scholarship, and (3) a final note on the art, craft, and science of ECB.

Toward Usable ECB Indicators

ECB, that is, the day-to-day effort to make evaluation studies and their uses possible, can begin with an assessment of organizational wants, needs, and dreams for evaluation. Included might be notions about how quality evaluation could contribute to the organization, where it could best fit into an organizational structure, and with which management practices it would fit. Little has been shared about doing and designing ECB. To meet this need, we propose a simple tool—a checklist for assessing ECB in an organization and, by extension, for planning an organization-based ECB effort. In constructing this tool, we reflected on our own practices, the case studies, and the literature. The result is the checklist, "ECB Indicators: A Practical Checklist for Site Assessment" (see Table 7.1).

A 3 × 3 matrix gives structure to the checklist, which contains the three structural elements of the overall ECB process, actual ECB practices, and ECB occupational orientation and practitioner role. The other three categories are new and are based on the reality of ECB work. We have learned that ECB occurs at an organization site and is dependent on that site for its content, shape, and actual practices. Thus the three categories of site structure, site culture, and site practices are included in the matrix. Grounding ECB to a site prevents reification, that is, ideas claiming to be activities, and focuses attention on "the ways things are done around here" now.

Basic to these early and suggestive indicators is the somewhat odd notion that ECB can be present and can be assessed, even when it is not identified or named as such. As intentional practice, ECB can become simply "how things are done around here" and can be called mainstreaming (from 2001 AEA Annual Meeting "Call for Proposals"), or organizational development, or a type of organizational learning (Preskill and Torres, 1999). Even the ECB practitioner may not name the overall process using these very words. This is indeed likely, given this early stage of attention to ECB, the limited explicit ECB literature, the minimal diffusion of ECB terminology, and the early stage of mapping the ECB family of similar processes and practices.

Because ECB is site-dependent, an ECB geography might someday be done; for example, types of sites might be examined. Details of the sites could then be presented using standard categories for analyzing sites such as formal organizations, communities, and governmental ministries. Details about ECB at that site would include whether and how site structures serve to make possible or hinder the carrying out of the ongoing work of doing and using quality program evaluation. At a minimum, it is necessary that there be a formal, occupational position with some sphere of authority and responsibility for intentional ECB practices, identifiable appropriate resources to carry out the work, and an identifiable ECB process. Along with these, there must be a supportive site culture with a common, positive, normative understanding given to ECB work as "this is how things should be

Table 7.1. ECB Indicators: A Practical Checklist for Site Assessment

	Site Structures (organization, program, community, nation)	Site Cultures	Site Practices
Overall Process	• Identifiable ECB process is in place. • Identifiable ECB position, role, and occupational orientation are in place. • Identifiable structures are in place for quality evaluation and its uses. • Identifiable and appropriate resources are at levels necessary and sufficient. • Identifiable ECB unit is appropriately located in organizational structure.	• ECB as a legitimate and useful organizational process • Explicit ECB ethos, language, and discourses • A common, positive understanding of ECB work as "how things should be done around here" • A cultural value of inclusiveness regarding a variety of disciplines and their conceptual frames • A cultural value of inclusiveness regarding involvement of all stakeholders	• ECB is made explicit; it is explained and promoted actively and appropriately throughout the site.
Actual Practices	• ECB practitioner is in place. • ECB practitioner is lead worker for ECB practices. • Appropriate ECB resources are allocated. • ECB process has explicit, public, executive support. • ECB strategy is identifiable. • Identifiable unit is responsible for creating, managing, and sustaining ECB. • ECB practitioner is "at the table" when decisions are made. • ECB practitioner facilitates necessary intra- and interorganizational practices. • ECB must be demand-responsive.	• Use of multidisciplinary practice • Implementation of transparent and participatory practice • Intentional effort to be inclusive of all relevant stakeholder voices • Working to create ongoing use of common ECB language and discourse for common understanding of the ECB process and how it works	• ECB work fits site realities—structure, culture, resources, politics, ideologies, and practices such as the ways work is done • Within the ECB process, evaluation studies are conducted in accordance with utility, feasibility, propriety, and accuracy standards (Joint Committee standards).
Occupational Orientation and Practitioner Role	• Orientation to ECB theory, process, and practices • Outward orientation toward potential collaborators • Orientation to intentional, responsive, reflective practice • Orientation to appropriately inclusive practice (age, sex, race, ethnicity) • Commitment in all work to the standards of utility, feasibility, propriety, and accuracy (Joint Committee standards) • Orienation to ECB work as ongoing learning and teaching about quality evaluation and its uses	• ECB practitioner works to transform the site culture composed of language, meanings, values, and discourses so it is supportive of the ECB process, including quality evaluation and its uses.	• ECB practitioner guides ECB work to fit site structure, culture, resources, politics, ideologies, and practices.

done around here." There must also be ECB activities that are seen as part of a larger process linking site goals, site activities, resources, and so on, to ongoing program evaluation and its uses. If these preconditions are in place, then it is reasonable to look at indicators for actual ECB practices.

The indicators presented show how ECB is being carried out, that is, operationalized. These indicators can be seen, touched, and counted; together they make ECB real.

Someone has to have responsibility for ECB, and the work can best be carried out within a specially constituted ECB practitioner role. That role consists of an orientation toward what the work is, expectations about how it should and could (and should not) be done, as well as understandings about related bodies of knowledge, notions of expertise, conceptions of the ideal incumbent, and social norms about appropriate affect, motives, and styles of work. Taken together, the ECB orientation and practitioner role is "ECB literacy," that is, more or less explicit ways of reading and acting at the site so as to bring about, sustain, and manage ongoing quality program evaluation and its uses.

The ECB indicators included in the checklist can be used to determine whether and to what extent the ECB process is present. We treat these indicators as a minimum beginning list and expect additions and refinement as more writing on ECB is published. These indicators may be most usefully implemented by considering each as a question, the answer to which provides the substance for assessment. For example, in the structural elements, the indicator "identifiable ECB process in place" becomes, "Is there an identifiable ECB process in place?" The related question is, "To what extent is the ECB process fully operational?"

Toward a Framework of ECB

Table 7.2 presents an initial framework of ECB. This framework is a summative statement of ECB taken from our work, the case studies, and the literature. It may be most useful as a mapping of ECB as a practice and as a field of study; it may be best used as a reference to return to for insights and conversation.

Five questions were used to create the framework:

What are the ECB structural elements?
What are the core ECB themes?
What are the basic ECB concepts?
What is the relevant ECB knowledge?
What are the basic ECB skill competencies?

As before, items in each cell were taken from the literature, the case studies, and our work. This is a preliminary framework that is open to radical questioning and revision. What is contained in this framework is what is known at this point. It represents ECB at a minimal level. Given the earlier data and discussions, we now integrate these, presenting little that is new.

What is new is in two authors' notes. Author Note 3 is a suggestive listing of metaphors explicit and implicit in the ECB literature, in the case studies, and in the ECB discourses.

Art, Craft, and Science of ECB: A Final Note

ECB is an emergent field of practice, with an emergent overall process, actual practices, occupational orientation, and practitioner roles that form the ECB structural elements. Aspects of ECB are artlike, craftlike, and sciencelike, and actual ECB practitioners have all three at hand; they use all three in their everyday work.

Getting at the art, craft, and science of ECB is like unscrambling an omelet. The omelet has to be sorted to get at what is the art, the craft, and the science of ECB!

The craftsperson knows how to produce a particular product or outcome, over and over again. The artist—a master, an expert in using materials, technique, and processes—knows how to go about producing whatever is envisioned and intended. The scientist, like them, knows how to go about producing knowledge as a product; using techniques, materials, and processes agreed upon by a collegial community as right and appropriate to the study at hand. More than the other two, the scientist is bound to normative ways of proceeding if the work is to be accepted by colleagues as "scientific."

In real work by actual persons, these three occupational orientations blur and overlap. The actual worker "responds." One task in research about ECB is to get at the real, actual orientations and related practices of everyday ECB work. This will be possible only if practitioners work reflectively, that is, become reflective practitioners. In its own way, the "reflective practitioner" is also an ideal-type (Argyris and Schön, 1976; Schön, 1983, 1987).

Reflective practice is basic to actual ECB. Such self-awareness allows the work's very complexity to be understood, while making planning and related intentional actions possible. As discussed by Schön (1983, 1987), the practitioner can (should) be reflective about the espoused theories of ECB practice, the theories in actual use doing ECB, and the "reflected theories" about what was done, how, and why. Without such ongoing reflection on one's ECB practice, it is almost impossible to work in the forest and on the trees simultaneously, to keep both in mind, to imagine the links between them, to envision near- to far-term outcomes of different strategies, to have the necessary double or dual vision referred to in the case studies and the text. Without such reflection, there can be no professional practice, no ethically responsible practice, no quality practice, because each of these depends on the practitioner knowing, being able to say, and telling why she thought as

Table 7.2. Toward a Framework of ECB

ECB Structural Elements	Core ECB Themes	Basic ECB Concepts	Relevant ECB Knowledge	Basic ECB Skill Competencies
Overall Process	• ECB is the intentional work to constantly co-create and co-sustain an overall process making quality evaluation and its uses routine in organizations and other systems. • ECB is different from evaluation practice. • ECB is a context-dependent practice. • ECB is a guided and ongoing process. • ECB is done collaboratively. • ECB is political. • ECB is consistent with the call to make evaluation useful, feasible, conducted in an ethically responsible way, and accurate (Joint Committee standards).	• Emergence • Developmental • Site learning • Intentional • Guided • Co-creating • Co-sustaining • Intra- and interorganization or program	• How to guide complex, changing, ECB process over the longer term • Quality program evaluation and its uses • How to work collaboratively	• Work with "bifocals, double vision," and on both the forest and in trees • Implement ECB ethos and philosophy • Teach evaluation process and uses • Transform site structures and cultures • Sustain a longer-term effort
Actual Practices	• Actual work is on both the forest and the trees, now and in the future, here and there (that is, on multiple horizons simultaneously). • ECB work is never completed. • ECB is a group work practice with teams, coalitions, and other forms of partnership.	• Intentionality • "Practice wisdom" • "Rules of thumb" • "Way things are done" • Political • Guiding • Collaborative • Quality work	• How to operationalize ECB philosophy • How to work with and transform site practices and cultures • How to work in highly complex organizations • How to implement ECB processes in constantly changing site environments	• Work in groups • Work collaboratively" • Work "politically" • Work with a process orientation • Ensure the conduct of quality evaluation • Work within and across organizational structures and cultures

Occupational Orientation and Practitioner Role	• Occupational orientation to ECB literacy, that is, know where at the site ECB work can be successful now and in the future. • Every opportunity now must be understood in relation to larger ECB processes and to envisioning how they influence the longer-term opportunities. • The ECB practitioner's orientation is to a longer-term, ongoing process of co-creation and co-sustenation rather than to completing discrete, isolated evaluation studies.	• "Gaze" • Now-later horizons • Here-there horizons • Specific-big picture • Ongoing and sustaining • Espoused theories, theories in use, and reflected theories • Expertise • Site politics • Working together	• Reflective practice, such as "reading the site" • Quality evaluation, as specified by the Joint Standards • Acceptable evaluation approaches and methods • Which disciplinary models have utility for ECB work at this site; how ECB can be assessed • Why knowledge about formal organizations, systems, politics, group work is basic	• Read the organization and intra- and interorganizational texts using various frames (site literacy). • Read groups and organizational units as cultural, social, and political forms. • Work reflectively and politically. • Know how to illuminate the possibilities and promise of quality evaluation. • Know how to discern what is important to work on now. • Know how to work piece by piece, keeping the big picture in mind, day after day (that is, persistence, endurance, and sense of humor). • Know how to prevent "existential burnout" (the loss of meaning about the purpose of ECB work).

she did and acted as she did in *each and every moment*. To be able to work in this way is an unachievable ideal; it is also an actual and potent ethical imperative. Working in this way gives heft to the meanings of professional, responsible, and accountable practice, whether in art, craft, or science. It is through such self-reflective practice that one can be appropriately and professionally supervised and held to account; through self-reflection the practitioner is a member of a professional community. Self-reflection is a source for one's own "personal theorizing" (Ross, Cornett, and McCutcheon, 1992); one can use it to transform "intuition" (Davis-Floyd and Arvidson, 1997) into "grounded" hunches and hypothesis (Strauss and Corbin, 1997), and for doing "action research" (Carson and Sumara, 1997). Each can self-evaluate practice and have it evaluated by others.

This volume is another step in finding, documenting, and assessing the reflective practice of the art, craft, and science of ECB—the overall process and its actual practices at this moment in late modernity (Mabry, 1997) when everything seems to be changing quickly toward directions that are, in ways, unforeseen. After the 2000 and 2001 AEA Annual Meetings on capacity building and "mainstreaming," the field is beginning to know the "practice wisdom" and "rules of thumb" of experienced ECB practitioners. To get to the level of documenting and understanding more richly and deeply the necessary "practical knowledge" (Nyiri and Smith, 1998), more case studies and conceptual papers are needed. This is now our collective responsibility—to make a home for ECB practice and scholarship within the family of evaluation practices.

Author Note 1

Max Weber's "ideal-type" strategy (Gerth and Mills, 1946) was used to construct a "purely artificial device" (Bensman and Lilienfeld, 1973) "of certain elements of reality into a logically precise conception" (Gerth and Mills, 1946, p. 59) that could be used heuristically for a particular study, for example, "Puritan ethic" and "economic man"—also artist, craftsperson, and scientist. These are three "ideal-type" occupational orientations, with associated knowledge, beliefs, expertise, authority, and power. Each ideal-type is a particular gaze—a way of seeing, interpreting, and making sense, with real-world, actual consequences, as when a police officer "sees" a threat to her person, a politician "sees" people as potential voters, an artist "sees" the possibilities and promise of a shape or a piece of wood, and a physician perceives illness in the color of the eyes and the sheen of the hair.

ECB practice is art-like, craft-like, and science-like, and the ECB practitioner has at hand all of these occupational orientations to use "as necessary" in each emergent moment. When we know all about this, we will know ECB practice, how it works. Until then, the ECB practitioner can adopt, use, and thereby make real each of these ideal-type orientations.

In the ideal-type art orientation, ECB work is aesthetic (Kupfer, 1983), an "art of working," in which the shapes and movements and sounds of "the scene" suggest "ways of responding" so as to try to produce one's vision of what "needs to be done" for program evaluation and its uses to be ongoing and mundane activities at this site. In the ideal-type craft orientation, what is going on at the site is read as another example, which is in some ways, both similar to and different from what has gone on before. "Practice wisdom" from long-time experiences with "moments like these" becomes the literacy to read these "goings on" as a decipherable text which, once understood, can be responded to in ways that have "worked before" and can be modified and tried again (Klemm and Schweiker, 1993). The ideal-type scientist is also explicit in her literacy and uses explicit scientific canonical theory and method in transparent and reproducible ways to work out more or less formal hunches as to "what is going on and why" and responds to these interpretations with "ways which have been shown effective in situations and with conditions like this one."

A phenomenology of lived-practice can be envisioned in which the worker's point of view and the worker's particular gaze can be described, along time dimensions, for example. This could serve to join the ideal-type to actual reflective practice.

Author Note 2

A word on the use of metaphors in ECB. Metaphors undergird, shape, and give substance to a field of practice and to inquiry about it. Attention to metaphors may be especially important when a field is being formalized as an emergent normative professional practice. "Capacity" and "construction" are the "root metaphors" (Brown, 1989) of ECB, and to use these is to understand ECB through these symbols, meanings, and images. Reflective practice requires that we make this explicit; a new literature is highly suggestive of how metaphors inform scholarship and professional practice (for example, Leary, 1990; Olds, 1992; Rosenblatt, 1994). Metaphor is the link to the final note on the art, craft, and science of ECB.

It may be useful to reflect on metaphors that suggest how ECB can be conceptualized and practiced. As we worked on the text, ECB became for us a *construction* and *building process,* one that is *developmental.* From engineering, electricity, and physiology we took *capacity;* from psychology (cognitive), *ability.* ECB overall is an *emergent* process, an *infinite* rather than a *finite game*—of new and emergent rules and players; ECB is *improvisational* jazz and dance more than formal ballet. Most of all, the ECB practitioner is like the circus performer who spins and balances simultaneously several plates on long poles—evaluation studies, small group meetings to use evaluation findings, reports to an agency on program effectiveness, "politics" between the evaluation unit, the fundraising staff, and the public relations group—seemingly all at once!

Author Note 3

There are several nonevaluation literatures useful to understanding and practicing ECB. The following suggestions are organized by the ECB structural elements:

Overall Process	Actual Practices	Occupational Orientation and Practitioner Role
Carse (1986)	Carson and Sumara (1997)	Bensman and Lilienfeld (1973)
Fillingham (1993)	Nyiri and Smith (1995)	Hogarth (2001)
Mabry (1997)	Pollo, Henley, and Thompson	Howard (1982)
Preskill and Torres	(1997)	Klemm and Schweiker (1993)
(1999)	White (1999)	MacDonald (1995)
		Schön (1983, 1987)
		Strauss and Corbin (1997)
		Velleman (1989)
		Winter (1989)

References

Argyris, C., and Schön, D. *Theory in Practice: Increasing Professional Effectiveness.* San Francisco: Jossey-Bass, 1976.

Bensman, J., and Lilienfeld, R. *Craft and Consciousness: Occupational Technique and the Development of World Images.* New York: Wiley, 1973.

Brown, R. *A Poetic for Sociology.* Chicago: University of Chicago Press, 1989.

Carse, J. *Finite and Infinite Games: A Vision of Life and Play as Possibility.* New York: Ballantine Books, 1986.

Carson, T., and Sumara, D. (eds.). *Action Research as a Living Practice.* New York: Peter Lang, 1997.

Davis-Floyd, R., and Arvidson, P. (eds.). *Intuition: The Inside Story.* New York: Routledge, 1997.

Fillingham, L. *Foucault for Beginners.* New York: Writers & Readers Publishing, 1993.

Gerth, H., and Mills, C. (eds.). *From Max Weber: Essays in Sociology.* New York: Oxford University Press, 1946.

Hogarth, R. *Educating Intuition.* Chicago: University of Chicago Press, 2001.

Howard, V. *Artistry: The Work of Artists.* Indianapolis: Hackett, 1982.

Joint Committee on Standards for Education Evaluation. *The Program Evaluation Standards.* (2nd ed.) Thousand Oaks, Calif.: Sage, 1994.

Klemm, D., and Schweiker, W. (eds.). *Meanings in Texts and Actions: Questioning Paul Ricoeur.* Charlottesville: University Press of Virginia, 1993.

Kupfer, J. *Experience as Art: Aesthetics in Everyday Life.* Albany, N.Y.: State University of New York Press, 1983.

Leary, D. (ed.). *Metaphors in the History of Psychology.* Cambridge, England: Cambridge University Press, 1990.

Mabry, L. (ed.). "Evaluation and the Postmodern Dilemma." In *Advances in Program Evaluation,* no. 3. Greenwich, Conn.: JAI Press, 1997.

MacDonald, K. *The Sociology of the Professions.* Thousand Oaks, Calif.: Sage, 1995.

Nyiri, J., and Smith, B. (eds.). *Practical Knowledge: Outlines of a Theory of Traditions and Skills.* London: Croom Helm, 1998.

Olds, L. E. *Metaphors of Interrelatedness.* Albany: State University of New York Press, 1992.

Pollio, H., Henley, R., and Thompson, C. *The Phenomenology of Everyday Life.* Cambridge: Cambridge University Press, 1997.

Preskill, H., and Torres, R. T. *Evaluative Inquiry for Learning in Organizations.* Thousand Oaks, Calif.: Sage, 1999.

Rosenblatt, P. *Metaphors of Family Systems Theory: Toward New Constructions.* New York: Guilford Press, 1994.

Ross, E., Cornett, J., and McCutcheon, G. (eds.). *Teacher Personal Theorizing: Connecting Curriculum Practice, Theory and Research.* Albany, N.Y.: State University of New York Press, 1992.

Schön, D. A. *The Reflective Practitioner.* New York: Basic Books, 1983.

Schön, D. A. *Educating the Reflective Practitioner.* San Francisco: Jossey-Bass, 1987.

Schön, D., and Rein, M. *Frame Reflection.* New York: Basic Books, 1994.

Strauss, A., and Corbin, J. (eds.). *Grounded Theory in Practice.* Thousand Oaks, Calif.: Sage, 1997.

Velleman, J. *Practical Reflection.* Princeton, N.J.: Princeton University Press, 1989.

White, J. *Taking Language Seriously: The Narrative Foundations of Public Administration Research.* Washington, D.C.: Georgetown University Press, 1999.

Winter, R. *Learning from Experience: Principles and Practice in Action Research.* London: The Falmer Press, 1989.

MICHAEL BAIZERMAN *is a professor in the School of Social Work and adjunct professor in the College of Education and Human Development and in the School of Public Health at the University of Minnesota, St. Paul.*

DONALD W. COMPTON *is director of the Division Evaluation Services, American Cancer Society, National Home Office, Atlanta.*

STACEY HUEFTLE STOCKDILL *is founder and CEO of EnSearch, Inc., a specialized evaluation firm in St. Paul, Minnesota.*

INDEX

Accountability: and ECB development, 49–50; and evaluation findings, 16; as learning tool, 19; of public sector, 29–30

Adrien, M. H., 85, 89

American Cancer Society study, 4, 20, 47–60, 106; aims of ECB in, 8, 47; assessment of ECB, 59; Cancer Control Department's role in, 49; context of, 48–51; and ECB practice principles, 53–58; ECB processes and practice in, 55–58; and ECB-CEFP structure and processes, 51–53, 54, 57; and fiscal accountability and stewardship demands, 49–50; funding for, 52; and lessons for researchers, 60; and NHO, 49, 50, 52, 55, 57; and UFE principles, 52, 53, 54, 58

American Evaluation Association (AEA), 4, 93; electronic discussion forum, 36; presidential strand on ECB, 41–42; President's Prize, 34

Anoka-Hennepin Independent School District 11 study, 4, 9, 63–79, 106; curriculum in, 77–78; ECB goals in, 68–74; evaluation practice framework in, 76–79; focus groups and self-study in, 69–71; internal evaluator's role in, 66–67, 68, 76; lessons learned from, 74–79; student assessment context of, 64–66

Argyris, C., 113

Arvidson, P., 116

Avery, M. E., 47

Baizerman, M., 7, 18, 52, 59, 101, 109

Baker, J. L., 84

Baker, Q. E., 40

Behavioral Risk Factor Surveillance System, 41

Bensman, H., 116

Boyle, R., 15

Brushet, S., 85

Carse, J., 13, 19

Carson, T., 116

CDC (Centers for Disease Control and Prevention) study, 4, 8, 20, 28–44, 106; accomplishments and lessons learned, 40–41; accountability in, 29–30, 35; documentation of findings in, 32, 37; evaluation agenda of, 30, 31–32; Evaluation Working Group in, 30–41; historical context of, 30–31; institutional change agenda in, 31–32, 34–35, 36–40; and public health trends, 35–36; and public health workers participation, 34–36

CDC *Framework for Program Evaluation in Public Health,* 27–28

Chapel, T. J., 27

Compton, D. W., 7, 18, 47, 52, 59, 101, 109

Conceptual framework of evaluation, 53

Concerns-Based Adoption Model Survey, 65

Conclusions on cases: common findings in, 104–107; and future research, 109–118

Corbin, J., 116

Cornett, J., 104, 116

Cotton, D., 4, 27, 28, 41

Culture, local, and ECB practice, 22

Data collection/analysis: infrastructure for, 69; in school program evaluation, 71–72

Davis-Floyd, R., 116

Definitions of ECB: conceptual, 8–9, 19, 95–97, 104–107; in ECB literature, 14–15; working, 1, 14

Development programs: and country–level ECD, 81, 86–93; and ECB's quality and evaluation focus, 96–97; evaluation literature on, 14–16; "Poverty Reduction Strategy Paper," 85; stakeholder base for ECB in, 17–18; UNDP mandates for, 17–18; and World Bank's ECD, 81–97

Donors: accountability demands of, 49–50; evaluation dominance of, 17–18; national, 16

Duhon-Sells, S. M., 18

Dyal, W. W., 27

Econometric model of demand, 19

Emory University's Rollins School of Public Health, 51–52, 58

Back Issue/Subscription Order Form

Copy or detach and send to:
Jossey-Bass, 989 Market Street, San Francisco CA 94103-1741

Call or fax toll free!
Phone 888-378-2537 6AM-5PM PST; Fax 800-605-2665

Back issues: Please send me the following issues at $27 each.
                 (Important: please include series initials and issue number, such as EV77.)

1. EV _____

_____

_____

$ _____ Total for single issues

$ _____ SHIPPING CHARGES: SURFACE   Domestic   Canadian

		Domestic	Canadian
First Item		$5.00	$6.00
Each Add'l Item		$3.00	$1.50

For next-day and second-day delivery rates, call the number listed above.

Subscriptions   Please ❑ start   ❑ renew my subscription to *New Directions for Evaluation* for the year ___ at the following rate:

U.S.	❑ Individual $69	❑ Institutional $145
Canada	❑ Individual $69	❑ Institutional $185
All Others	❑ Individual $93	❑ Institutional $219

$ _____ Total single issues and subscriptions (Add appropriate sales tax for your state for single issue orders. No sales tax for U.S. subscriptions. Canadian residents, add GST for subscriptions and single issues.)

❑ Payment enclosed (U.S. check or money order only.)

❑ VISA, MC, AmEx, Discover Card #_____ Exp. date_____

Signature _____ Day phone _____

❑ Bill me (U.S. institutional orders only. Purchase order required.)

Purchase order #_____

Name _____

Address _____

_____

Phone_____ E-mail _____

For more information about Jossey-Bass, visit our Web site at:
www.josseybass.com   **PRIORITY CODE = ND1**

CALL FOR NOMINATIONS
for the editorship of
New Directions in Evaluation
term begins January 2003

The publications committee of the American Evaluation Association invites nominations for the editorship of *New Directions for Evaluation*. The journal aims to attain a broad coverage of topics of interest to all evaluators and to encourage reflection on evaluation. NDE publishes empirical, methodological, and theoretical works on all aspects of evaluation.

Responsibilities and duties include soliciting proposals for guest-edited issues, accepting and rejecting proposals and manuscripts based on their quality and suitability for NDE, guiding volumes through the review process, overseeing revisions, and working with the publisher on production matters. The publisher is responsible for all production aspects of NDE. The publisher provides a modest editorial fee of $800 per year to cover the costs of postage, telephone, photocopy and other direct expenses.

Nominees should be recognized scholars in evaluation. Nominees should also possess good managerial and organizational skills. Self-nominations and nominations of others are welcome, as are nominations for coeditors or editorial teams.

The deadline for nominations is June 15, 2002. Appointment of the new editor will be made no later than November 2002.

Send letters of nomination to

Susan Kistler
AEA Manager
16 Sconticut Neck Rd #290
Fairhaven, MA 02719